Dedication

To my favorite people to celebrate—my family

Acknowledgments

My wholehearted thanks goes to Amy Marson and the entire team at C&T Publishing—my editors Michele Fry, Joanna Burgarino, Alison Schmidt, Katie Van Amburg, and Nan Powell; my book designer Katie McIntosh and cover designer Kristy Zacharias; the photography team of Nissa Brehmer, Diane Pedersen, and Mary Peyton Peppo; production coordinator Freesia Pearson Blizard; illustrator Jenny Davis; and of course Roxane Cerda and Gailen Runge.

Also thanks to the wonderful companies that manufacture the fabrics that I used to create the pieces for this book: Art Gallery Fabrics, Blend Fabrics, Riley Blake Fabrics, and Robert Kaufman Fabrics. The talented designers whose fabrics I was fortunate enough to play with are listed in Resources (page 110).

A heartfelt thanks goes to Aurifil and the Warm Company. Aurifil threads come in a wonderful array of colors and are such a pleasure with which to sew! All the quilts feature Warm & White batting—my favorite!

And last but not least I'd like to thank BERNINA. It is a pleasure to sew each and every stitch using your wonderful machines. Thanks for your support.

CONTENTS

INTRODUCTION

It is always wonderful to celebrate the milestones in life with a quilt—something that will last and commemorate the event. As quilters, we are fortunate that we are able to express our love for those around us with needle and thread. This book is full of sophisticated and modern designs to help you commemorate life's memorable, special moments and milestones. I hope you will enjoy making these quilts as much as I've enjoyed designing them.

I have designed a quilt top and a quilt back for each project, which allows you to easily personalize them. You can piece the front design, the back design, or both! Each quilt back design is 5″ larger in each direction than the quilt top design, allowing it to be mounted on a quilting machine with ease. (Make sure to center the top over it for a clean finish!) Each back design also features an area to personalize the quilt with a special message. You can read more ideas for how to do this in Personalizing Your Quilts (pages 7–13).

I hope you enjoy making memories through quilting for the special people in your life!

Happy quilting!

—Amanda

Personalizing Your Quilts

There are so many ways to personalize a quilt. For a quilt that commemorates one of life's exceptional moments, personalization is especially important. I chose to customize the quilt backs in this book while keeping the fronts understated; however, there is no reason that you can't piece a back design and use it for the front of a quilt if you desire! (Keep in mind that the quilt backs are designed to be 5˝ larger on each side than the fronts, so if you use the back design for the front, the finished size of your quilt will be different from the size listed in the project.) All the methods presented in this chapter can be used interchangeably on the different designs.

Whatever your tools of choice, use your imagination and make the quilts in *Quilted Celebrations* your own!

LESLEY RILEY'S TAP TRANSFER ARTIST PAPER

One quick and easy way to personalize a quilt is to use Lesley Riley's TAP Transfer Artist Paper (from C&T Publishing) and an inkjet printer. This paper allows you to print any image on the printer and then transfer the image onto fabric using your iron! I found I had the best results transferring dark letters to light fabric rather than vice versa. To personalize using TAP, follow these steps:

1. Arrange your message in a word-processing or image-editing program, and print out a test on printer paper. You may need to put the words on different lines to fit. Lay the words on your quilt to check the font size. (Most of the characters I used for these quilts were between 160 and 200 points.)

2. Once you're happy with the appearance of your message, use your computer program or printer settings to invert the text. Print out the inverted text on the transfer paper. Figure 1

3. Cut out the message from the transfer paper about ⅛" from the edge of the letters. This often works better than simply cutting a rectangle around the words because the blank areas can leave a bit of film that might show on very light fabrics. Figure 2

4. Following the manufacturer's directions, transfer the image to your fabric using an iron. Figure 3

5. Touch up any areas with fabric paint, if desired. Figure 4

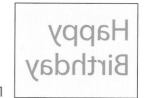

1

2

Cutting out letters

3

Fusing transfer to fabric

Happy Birthday

4

Finished transfer

On the back of *Flora* (page 26), this special message, created with TAP, celebrates the day.

> **TIP**
>
> For more TAP tips and ideas, consult Lesley Riley's book *Create with Transfer Artist Paper* (from C&T Publishing).

HANDWRITING

When you would like to have a group of people involved in creating the finished message, fabric markers are a great way to go. Fabrico pens were used to memorialize special recollections in *We Remember…* (page 94) and they were used again to create an autographed area for the alternative back panel of *Congratulations, Grad!* (page 62). The Essential Sandboard by Piece O' Cake Designs (from C&T Publishing) is a great tool to have on hand to keep the fabric from slipping when working with fabric pens. Remember to follow any specific instructions from the manufacturer to set the ink if necessary.

EMBROIDERY

Hand Embroidery

Hand embroidery is also an option for recording an event. You can embroider over handwritten letters or you can print out letters on a computer and trace them onto the fabric using a lightbox or window. The options are endless.

Machine Embroidery

If you are lucky enough to own a sewing machine that can also embroider, machine embroidery is a great option for personalization. Letters created with machine embroidery have a polished look that is unmatched. Bring out the color in your fabric by choosing a fun thread. Light colors can look beautiful on dark fabrics when using this method. *Welcome to the World!* (page 16), *Congratulations, Grad!* (page 62), *A Life Together* (page 82), and *I Do!* (page 72) all feature machine embroidery.

On the back of *We Remember…*, lettering done with fabric markers commemorates wonderful memories.

Machine embroidery records the recipient's name on the back of *Welcome to the World!*

APPLIQUÉ

And last, but not least, is fusible appliqué. It is among my favorite techniques and I use it to create design elements in quilts that could not be achieved with piecing alone. I also use fusible appliqué as a customizable element, both in the large numbers on the back of *Celtic Knot* (page 34), a sophisticated birthday quilt, and to mark an anniversary on the front of *A Life Together* (page 82). For more appliqué tips, check out my Craftsy (craftsy.com) appliqué class (see Resources, page 110).

On the back of *Celtic Knot* (page 34), large appliqué numbers commemorate a birthday.

SOME THOUGHTS ABOUT QUILTING

There are many ways to quilt any quilt, and no one way is right. In fact, more often than not, I wish I had time to make multiple versions of the same quilt top so that I could try them all!

When you have a lot of intricacy in the piecing, a simple overall design is a great choice. I chose an allover floral design for *Flora* (page 26) and a hard-edged square pattern for *Celtic Knot* (page 34) so that the shapes in the design of the quilt top would be echoed in the quilting. My good friend Cherry Guidry did the quilting on these pieces, and I couldn't be happier with the results!

An allover pantograph quilting design by Sweet Dreams Quilt Studio on *Flora* (page 26)

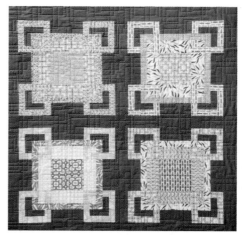

A very different allover pantograph design, also by Sweet Dreams Quilt Studio, on *Celtic Knot* (page 34)

In *Blessings* (page 44), I took
that concept one step further
and quilted crosses in a variety
of sizes in the background of the
main motif. Then I filled in the
negative space with a heart-shaped
paisley and pebble design that
mimicked my Topiary fabrics in
the background. Quilts with lots
of negative space give so much
freedom to the quilter—take
advantage of it!

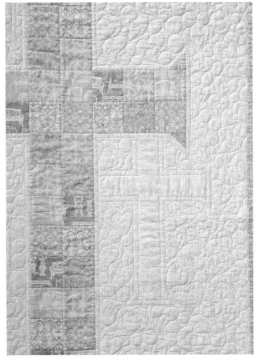

Quilted cross designs add interest and texture in
an understated way in the background of *Blessings*
(page 44).

In *I Do!* (page 72), I took quilting inspiration from the appliqué shapes.
Paisley hearts and feathers seem to spring from the central motifs and
stand out from the solid dark-gray background, giving a modern feel to
a very traditional design.

Modern and traditional styles are blended in *I Do!* (page 72)

The multiple borders of *I Do!* create opportunities to play with various quilting patterns as well.

The realistic birds in *A Life Together* (page 82) are set off by an abstract prism background. Blending the modern and the traditional is always interesting...and fun!

Birds rest on a branch against a crackled sky in *A Life Together* (page 82).

Sometimes inspiration can come from the fabric itself. In *Congratulations, Grad!* (page 62), I took my cues from the swirling designs of my Modern Lace fabric line.

Swirls and lacy shapes coordinate with the fabrics in *Congratulations, Grad!* (page 62)

Most of the quilts in this book were quilted on a domestic machine—the BERNINA 780—so don't be intimidated by the quilting process. Go ahead and try your hand at free-motion quilting!

I love free-motion quilting, but sometimes a quilt can benefit from the simplicity that straight-line quilting provides. Reinforcing the vertical movement in *We Remember...* (page 94) seemed like a natural choice.

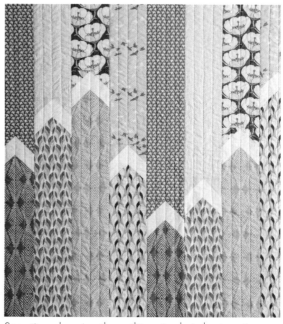

Sometimes keeping the quilting simple is best, as in *We Remember...* (page 94)

And other times, it is best to just let the quilting take on a life of its own. Deborah Norris quilted *Welcome to the World!* (page 16) in her light-hearted style that always makes me smile.

In *Welcome to the World!* (page 16), the buoyant waves and playful swirl shapes are just right for a nursery.

Remember, each quilt can be quilted in many different ways, and no single option is the only right one. So get out your free-motion (or walking) foot and a practice quilt sandwich and have fun!

> **TIP**
>
> For more free-motion quilting ideas, check out my *Free-Motion Quilting Idea Book* (from C&T Publishing).

General Instructions

- Seam allowances for all the projects in this book are ¼″ unless otherwise noted.

- *WOF* stands for width of fabric.

- All required yardage is based on a fabric width of 40″ to account for the trimming of selvages and shrinkage if the fabric is prewashed.

- A fat quarter refers to a ¼-yard piece of fabric approximately 18″ × 21″ that has been obtained by cutting 1 yard of fabric in half once on its length and once again on its width.

- The material requirements for the quilt tops and the quilt backs are listed separately in each project to make it easy for you to choose to make one or the other, not necessarily both.

- Each quilt back design is 5″ larger in each direction than its corresponding quilt top design so that it can be mounted to a longarm sewing machine with ease. Make any necessary adjustments if you make a top a back, make a back a top, use two backs, or any other combination you choose to make it your own.

- For more detailed tips on appliqué and finishing, refer to Tips and Techniques (page 104).

Commemorative Projects

Welcome to the World!

Brighten any nursery with this whimsical baby quilt!

QUILT TOP MATERIALS

- Block fabrics: ¾ yard each of 10 prints
- Background fabric: 2¼ yards white solid
- Animal fabric: ⅔ yards white solid
- Binding fabric: ⅝ yard
- Batting: 67″ × 81″
- Appliqué thread, 28 weight: black or dark coordinating color
- Temporary spray adhesive (See Tip, page 19.)
- Tear-away stabilizer: 12 sheets 15″ × 24″ (such as OESD Tear Away)*
- Disappearing-ink fabric marker

* If you don't have larger sheets of stabilizer on hand, you can use smaller sheets and overlap them a bit so that they back the entire appliqué area. If you prefer not to use stabilizer, you can heavily starch the background fabric.

QUILT TOP CUTTING INSTRUCTIONS

From the block fabrics:

From each print:

Cut 1 strip 2½″ × WOF. Subcut each strip in half to yield 2 pieces 2½″ × 20″. Set aside these strips to use for the checkered border.

From the remaining yardage:

Cut a *total* of 6 squares 13″ × 13″ and 3 rectangles 13″ × 27″ from the various prints.

Cut a variety of circles 9″, 7″, 5″, and 3″ in diameter using either the circle patterns (pullout page P1), a compass, circle cutter, or round objects of a similar size. (You'll need about 60 circles total for the quilt top and back, but you can always go back and cut additional circles as you need them.)

From the background solid:

Cut 7 strips 4½″ × WOF. Piece 2 rectangles 4½″ × 56½″ and 2 rectangles 4½″ × 62½″ for the outer border.

Cut 11 strips 2½″ × WOF. Piece 8 of the strips into 2 rectangles 2½″ × 44½″ for the inner border and 4 rectangles 2½″ × 54½″ for the inner border and sashing.

Subcut the remaining 3 strips into 6 rectangles 2½″ × 12½″ for sashing and 8 rectangles 2½″ × 2¼″ for the checkered borders.

Cut 6 strips 2″ × WOF. Cut each strip into 2 pieces 2″ × 20″ for the checkered borders.

From the binding fabric:

Cut 7 strips 2¼″ × WOF.

WOF = width of fabric

FINISHED QUILT: 56½″ × 70½″

Pieced by Amanda Murphy and quilted by Deborah Norris

Animal Block Assembly

1. Trace 1 of each of the 4 animals (pullout page P2) onto the right side of the white solid using a water-soluble or heat-removable pen. Be sure to trace lightly—you want it to be easy to cover the lines with machine stitching! Cut out the animals. Set aside the remaining white solid for the animal on the quilt back.

2. Lightly trace the animal details (the eyes, ears, nose, and the monkey's hair) onto the right side of the print fabrics for the blocks. Cut out the details.

3. Spray the back of the animal and the animal detail shapes with temporary spray adhesive, and then position them on the 4 squares 13″ × 13″. The bottom raw edge of the animal should align with the bottom raw edge of the block.

4. Refer to Tips and Techniques (page 104) to back the blocks with tear-away stabilizer and, using a blanket stitch and 28-weight thread, secure the edge of the shapes. Outline the animal details by using a triple stitch, going back and forth with machine stitching, or even hand stitching. Remove the stabilizer.

5. Trim the blocks to 12½″ × 12½″.

Animal block

TIP

I opted to trace these animals and secure them using temporary spray adhesive because of their large size. For this reason, the animal templates on the insert are not reversed. If you are sewing with dark background fabrics, you can opt to use paper-backed fusible web to trace the animals using a windowing technique (see Appliqué Basics, page 104) instead of using temporary spray adhesive. If you aren't using the temporary spray adhesive, make sure to trace a mirror-image of the animals included on the pullout if you would like the finished result to be like the original. Also, be careful not to set in any water-soluble pen markings by going over them with your iron! Windowing the fusible will allow you to cut away the background fabric from behind the animal appliqués so that it doesn't show through.

Circle Block Assembly

1. Arrange the circles on the remaining 2 print 13″ × 13″ squares and 3 rectangles 13″ × 27″. Feel free to have the circles overlap the edges of the fabric for added interest. When you are pleased with the arrangement, spray the back of each circle with temporary spray adhesive and reposition each one on the blocks.

2. Back the blocks with tear-away stabilizer and, using a blanket stitch and 28-weight thread, secure the edges of the shapes.

3. Trim the blocks to 12½″ × 12½″ and 12½″ × 26½″, respectively.

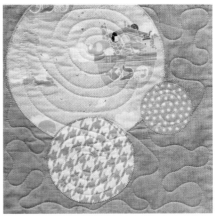

Circle block

Checkered Border Assembly

1. Join 1 print strip 2½″ × 20″ to 1 background strip 2″ × 20″. Repeat to make a total of 12 strip sets. Cut 6 assorted squares 2½″ × 2½″ from the remaining print strips and set aside.

Checkered border strip set

Cut 5 units 2½″ wide from each strip set.

2. Join 15 of the units from Step 1 to form the checkered border for the side of the quilt top. Join 1 print 2½″ × 2½″ square onto 1 end of the border, continuing the checkered pattern. Then join a background 2½″ × 2¼″ rectangle onto each end of the border. Repeat to make the other side border.

Hint

If your borders aren't quite big enough because of all the piecing, use slightly longer background pieces at the ends of each border to make up the difference. No one will ever know!

Side checkered border

3. Join 11 of the units from Step 1 together to form the top checkered border. Join 1 print 2½″ × 2½″ square on 1 end of the border, continuing the checkered pattern. Then join a background 2½″ × 2¼″ rectangle and a print 2½″ × 2½″ square onto each end of the border. Repeat to make the bottom checkered border.

Top and bottom checkered borders

Quilt Top Assembly

1. Following the quilt top assembly diagram (below), join 2 blocks 12½″ × 12½″, 1 block 12½″ × 26½″, and 2 background rectangles 2½″ × 12½″ to form a column. Repeat to make all 3 columns.

2. Join a background rectangle 2½″ × 54½″ between each of the 3 columns to form the center of the quilt top. Then join an additional rectangle on either side for the inner border.

3. Join a background rectangle 2½″ × 44½″ to the top and bottom of the quilt top.

4. Join the longer checkerboard borders to both sides of the quilt top.

5. Join the shorter checkerboard borders to the top and bottom of the quilt top.

6. Join a background rectangle 4½″ × 62½″ to the sides of the quilt top.

7. Join a background rectangle 4½″ × 56½″ to the top and bottom of the quilt top.

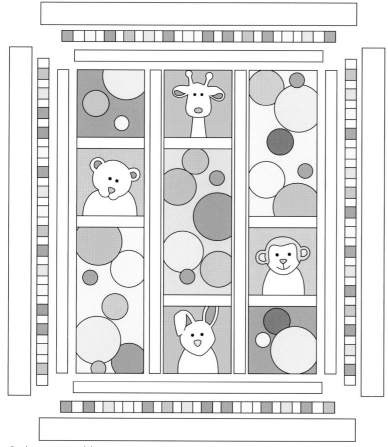

Quilt top assembly

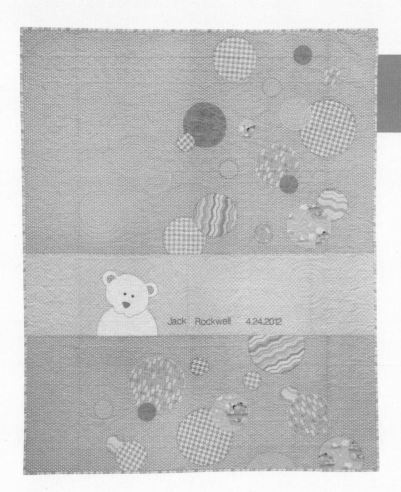

QUILT BACK

66½″ × 80½″ unfinished
(5″ larger on all sides than
the quilt top)

Bubbles of fun prints float
up the back of this quilt!

QUILT BACK MATERIALS

- Circles and animal fabric left over from
making the quilt top
- Background fabric: 4¼ yards
- Middle stripe fabric: 1 yard
- Appliqué thread, 28 weight: black or dark
coordinating color
- Paper-backed fusible web: ½ yard, 18″ wide
- Tear-away stabilizer: ½ yard or 1 sheet*,
15″ × 24″
- Tools for personalization (pages 8–10)

*If you don't have larger sheets of stabilizer on hand, you
can use smaller sheets and overlap them a bit so that they
back the entire appliqué area. If you prefer not to use
stabilizer, you can heavily starch the background fabric.*

QUILT BACK CUTTING INSTRUCTIONS

From the background fabric:

Cut 2 strips 40½″ × WOF. Subcut into 1 rectangle
40½″ × 40″ and 2 rectangles 40½″ × 13¾″. Join the
smaller rectangles to each side of the large rectangle
to yield a pieced rectangle 40½″ × 66½″.

Cut 2 strips 27½″ × WOF. Subcut into 1 rectangle
27½″ × 40″ and 2 rectangles 27½″ × 13¾″. Join the
smaller rectangles to each side of the large rectangle
to yield a pieced rectangle 27½″ × 66½″.

From the middle stripe fabric:

Cut 2 strips 13½″ × WOF. Subcut into 1 rectangle
13½″ × 40″ and 2 rectangles 13½″ × 13¾″. Join the
smaller rectangles to each side of the large rectangle
to yield a pieced rectangle 13½″ × 66½″.

WOF = width of fabric

Appliqué

1. Trace and appliqué your favorite animal to the middle stripe rectangle, following the instructions in Animal Block Assembly (page 19). Be sure to align the bottom raw edge of the animal with the bottom raw edge of the rectangle and position the left edge of the animal 16″ from the left edge of the rectangle.

2. Using the quilt back assembly diagram for placement, trace and appliqué the circles following the instructions in Circle Block Assembly (page 20) to the background. As you're arranging, remember that anything coming within 5″ of the raw edges of the sides of the quilt backing will be cut off after the quilting is complete!

Personalization

Record the new baby's name and date of birth next to the animal on the stripe using the technique in Lesley Riley's TAP Transfer Artist Paper (page 8), fabric pens, or machine or hand embroidery. (I used 150-point type.) *Remember to place text at least ¼″ from all outer edges so it will not be lost in the seam allowances.*

Quilt Back Assembly

1. Join the larger background rectangle to the top of the stripe.

2. Join the smaller background rectangle to the bottom of the stripe.

Finishing

Refer to Finishing Basics (page 108) for more detailed instructions.

1. Layer the backing, batting, and quilt top. Quilt as desired.

2. Join the 2¼″ × WOF binding strips into 1 continuous piece for binding. Press, folding the strip in half lengthwise. Sew the binding to the quilt using your preferred method.

Change It Up

This quilt welcomes a new addition to a family, but it's appropriate as well for a toddler's birthday (if you happen to miss the birth)! It also lends itself to a wonderful nursery or kid's room decoration, such as the Baby Safari Wallhangings (page 24).

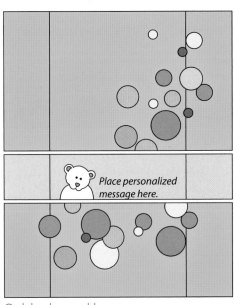

Place personalized message here.

Quilt back assembly

BABY SAFARI WALLHANGINGS

Finished Wallhanging: 12″ × 12″

Fabrics shown are from the Splendor collection by Lila Tueller for Riley Blake Designs and Basics by Riley Blake Designs.

Mount the appliquéd blocks onto artist's canvas for adorable, personalized wall art. Bold background prints are particularly fun!

WALLHANGING MATERIALS

- Backgrounds: ½ yard from each of 4 fabrics (Large, graphic prints work particularly well.)

- Animals: ⅔ yard white solid or white-on-white prints

- Animal details: Scraps from small-scale coordinating prints

- Appliqué thread, 28 weight: Black or dark coordinating color

- Temporary spray adhesive

- Tear-away stabilizer: 2 yards 18″ wide, or 4 sheets* 15″ × 24″

- Batting: 4 squares 12″ × 12″

- 4 artist's canvases mounted on 12″ × 12″ frames

- Staples and staple gun

If you don't have larger sheets of stabilizer on hand, you can use smaller sheets and overlap them a bit so that they back the entire appliqué area. If you prefer not to use stabilizer, you can heavily starch the background fabric.

CUTTING INSTRUCTIONS

From *each* background fabric:

Cut a square 17″ × 17″.

ced by Amanda Murphy

Animal Block Assembly

1. Refer to the Tip (page 19) to trace the animals (pullout page P2) onto the right side of the white fabric using a water-soluble or heat-removable pen, allowing an extra 2″ margin at the bottom of each animal to wrap around the artist's canvas for a clean finish. Trace lightly—you want it to be easy to cover the lines with machine stitching! Cut out the animals.

2. Lightly trace the animal details (including the eyes, ears, nose, and the monkey's hair) onto the right side of the small-scale coordinating prints. Cut out the details.

3. Spray the back of the animals and animal detail shapes with temporary spray adhesive and then position on the blocks. The bottom raw edge of the animal should align with the bottom raw edge of the block.

4. Refer to Tips and Techniques (page 104) to back the blocks with tear-away stabilizer and, using a blanket stitch and 28-weight thread, secure the edge of the shapes. Outline the animal details by using a triple blanket stitch, going back and forth with machine stitching or even hand stitching. Remove the stabilizer.

Finishing

1. Using temporary spray adhesive, attach a 12″ × 12″ square of batting to the front of a canvas-covered frame.

2. Place the block right side down on a clean surface. Center the frame, batting side down, on top of the block. Wrap the fabric around to the back of the frame, mitering the corners. Staple the fabric to secure it.

3. Repeat the entire process to complete 4 wallhangings.

Flora

Celebrate her birthday with a floral explosion of color! For a quick finish, one row of this quilt would make a great runner for a bed or table.

QUILT TOP MATERIALS

- Flower and piano key strip fabrics: 1 yard each of 11 prints
- Appliqué background: 2¼ yards
- Narrow border: ¾ yard
- Wide borders: ⅝ yard
- Binding: ⅝ yard
- Batting: 65″ × 87″
- Appliqué thread, 28 weight: in coordinating colors
- Paper-backed fusible web: 12 yards (or temporary fusible spray adhesive) 18″ wide
- Tear-away stabilizer: 10 sheets* 15″ × 24″, or 5½ yards 18″ wide

If you don't have larger sheets of stabilizer on hand, you can use smaller sheets and overlap them a bit so that they back the entire appliqué area. If you prefer not to use stabilizer, you can heavily starch the background fabric.

QUILT TOP CUTTING INSTRUCTIONS

From *each* of the flower prints:

Cut 5 strips 2½″ × WOF for the piano keys. Set aside the remaining fabric to use for appliqué flowers.

From the appliqué background fabric:

Cut 5 strips 15″ × WOF. Piece into 3 rectangles 15″ × 55½″.

From the narrow border fabric:

Cut 15 strips 1½″ × WOF. Piece 6 rectangles 1½″ × 54½″.

Piece 4 rectangles 1½″ × 64½″ and set them aside for the quilt back.

From the wide border fabric:

Cut 6 strips 3″ × WOF. Piece 4 rectangles 3″ × 54½″.

From the binding fabric:

Cut 8 strips 2¼″ × WOF.

WOF = width of fabric

FINISHED QUILT: 54½″ × 76½″

Fabrics shown are from the Bella collection by Amanda Murphy for Blend Fabrics.

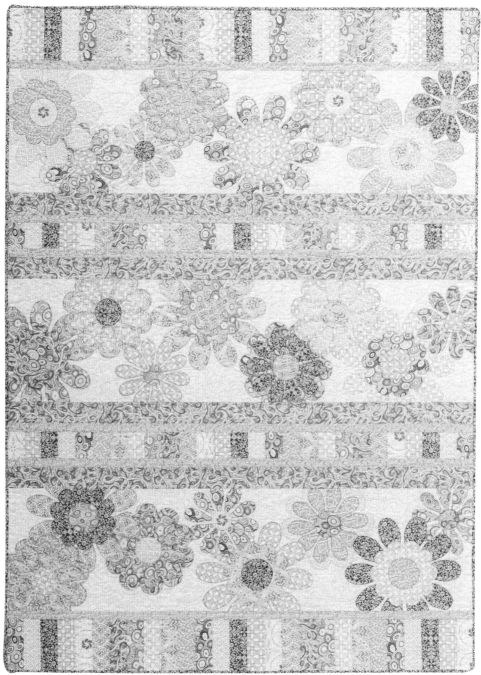

Pieced by Amanda Murphy; quilted by Cherry Guidry using Pretty Whimsy Panto 002 by Sweet Dreams Quilt Studio

Piano Key Strip Set Assembly

1. Join together 1 strip 2½" × WOF of each of the 11 flower prints for the piano keys. Press the seams open. Repeat this step to form 2 identical strip sets. Then cut 2 units 6½" wide and 2 units 3½" wide from each set. Set aside the remainder of the strip sets—they will be used later in the quilt back. **Figure 1**

2. Join together 5 more piano key strips 2½" × WOF, pressing the seams open. Cut 2 units 6½" wide and 2 units 3½" wide from this set. Set aside the remainder of the strip set to use on quilt back. **Figure 2**

3. Join 2 long and 1 short 6½"-wide units together to form 2 strips with 27 piano keys each. **Figure 3**

4. Join 2 long and 1 short 3½"-wide units together to form 2 strips with 27 piano keys each. **Figure 4**

5. Join a narrow border 1½" × 54½" rectangle to the long sides of each of the 3½" piano key rows. Press the seams toward the narrow borders. **Figure 5**

6. Join a wide border 3" × 54½" rectangle to the long sides of the rows from Step 5. Press the seams toward the wide borders. **Figure 6**

7. Join a narrow border 1½" × 54½" rectangle to a single side of the 6½"-wide piano key rows. **Figure 7**

Appliqué

1. Following the instructions in Appliqué Basics (page 104), trace an assortment of Flora appliqué flowers (pullout page P1) onto the smooth side of paper-backed fusible web. (I traced 10 large flowers, 10 medium flowers, and 7 small flowers; then I set aside 1 of each to use on the back of the quilt.) Note that you should trace each part of the flower shapes separately, even though they overlap on the pullout. For example, to make a medium flower you should trace the flower center, inner petal shape, and outer petal shape as 3 separate pieces. Window the fusible (page 105), if desired, for large areas to ensure that the finished piece remains soft.

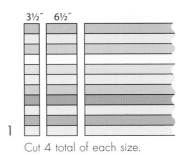

3½" 6½"

1

Cut 4 total of each size.

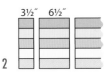

3½" 6½"

2

Cut 2 of each size.

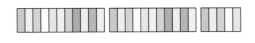

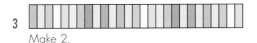

3

Make 2.

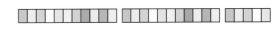

4

Make 2.

5

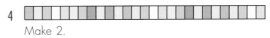

6

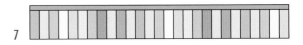

7

8

2. Fuse the rough side of the fusible flower shapes onto the wrong side of the flower fabrics. Cut out the flowers on the traced line.

3. Following the quilt top assembly diagram (below), arrange flowers on the appliqué background rectangles. (Note: Save any extra flowers for the quilt back.) Photograph the quilt to refer to your layout again.

4. Remove the paper and fuse the bottom layer of petals of each flower to temporarily secure them to the block.

You want to appliqué the bottom layer of petals first so that you can travel around the entire flower without having to start and stop threads between each petal. Use an appliqué pressing sheet or Silicone Release Paper (from C&T Publishing) under any flowers that extend beyond the edge of the background fabric to protect your ironing board from fusible residue.

5. Back the block with stabilizer and secure the appliqué shapes to the central panel using a blanket stitch. Refer to Appliqué Basics (page 104) as necessary.

6. Continue to fuse and appliqué the additional layers of each flower until you have finished the panels.

7. Trim the appliqué panels to 14½" × 54½". Figure 8

Quilt top assembly

Quilt Top Assembly

Join the 3 appliqué blocks to the piano key rows as shown in the quilt assembly diagram, at left.

QUILT BACK

64½″ × 86½″ unfinished
(5″ larger on all sides than
the quilt top)

Use the extra flower
appliqués from the
quilt top to create a
personalized bouquet
for the birthday girl!

QUILT BACK MATERIALS

- Flower appliqués set aside from the quilt top
- Narrow border rectangles 1½″ × 64½″ set aside from the quilt top
- Strip sets and remaining 2½″ strips set aside from the quilt top
- Top background fabric: 2½ yards
- Bottom background fabric: 1¼ yards
- Tools for personalization (pages 8–10)
- Tear-away stabilizer: 1 or 2 sheets* 15″ × 24″
- Appliqué thread, 28 weight: in coordinating colors

QUILT BACK CUTTING INSTRUCTIONS

From the top background fabric:

- Cut 2 strips 40½″ × WOF. Subcut into 1 rectangle 40½″ × 40″ and 2 rectangles 40½″ × 12¾″.

From the bottom background fabric:

- Cut 2 strips 17½″ × WOF. Subcut into 1 rectangle 17½″ × 40″ and 2 rectangles 17½″ × 12¾″.

WOF = width of fabric

If you don't have larger sheets of stabilizer on hand, you can use smaller sheets and overlap them a bit so that they back the entire appliqué area. If you prefer not to use stabilizer, you can heavily starch the background fabric.

Piano Key Strip Set Assembly

1. Join together 1 strip 2½″ × WOF of each of the 11 flower prints for the piano keys. Press the seams open. Cut a total of 4 units 11½″ wide and 2 units 3½″ wide from these sets plus the leftover set from making the quilt top.

2. Join together 10 more piano key 2½″ × WOF strips. Press the seams open. Cut 2 units 11½″ wide and 1 unit 3½″ wide from this set.

3. Join together 2 long and 1 short 11½″-wide units to form 2 strips with 32 piano keys each.

4. Join together 2 long and 1 short 3½″-wide units to form 1 strip with 32 piano keys.

5. Join a narrow border 1½″ × 64½″ rectangle to both long sides of the 3½″ piano key row. Press the seams toward the narrow borders.

Make 1.

6. Join a narrow border 1½″ × 64½″ rectangle to a single side of each 11½″ piano key row.

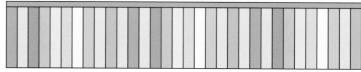

Make 2.

Quilt Back Assembly

1. Join 1 top background 40½″ × 12¾″ rectangle to each side of the top background 40½″ × 40″ rectangle.

2. Join 1 bottom background 17½″ × 12¾″ rectangle to each side of the top background 17½″ × 40″ rectangle.

3. Following the quilt back assembly diagram (page 33), join the background rectangles and piano key rows.

Personalization

Refer to Personalizing Your Quilts (page 7) to add your unique message using the method of your choice. For this quilt, I used Lesley Riley's TAP Transfer Artist Paper. Refer to the quilt assembly diagram (below) to place and apply the message on the quilt back. *Remember to place text at least ¼″ from all outer edges so it will not be lost in the seam allowances.*

Appliqué

1. Following the quilt back assembly diagram, arrange the appliqué shapes on the quilt back, at least 10″ from the edges of the quilt back.

2. Repeat Appliqué Basics, Steps 4–6 (page 105), to back with tear-away stabilizer and secure the appliqué shapes to the quilt back using a blanket stitch.

Finishing

Refer to Finishing Basics (page 108) for more detailed instructions.

1. Layer the backing, batting, and quilt top. Quilt as desired.

2. Join the 2¼″ × WOF binding strips into 1 continuous piece for binding. Press, folding the strip in half lengthwise. Sew the binding to the quilt using your preferred method.

Change It Up

These flowers might be just the style of a girl you know who is graduating, and an enlarged flower could easily replace the star on *Congratulations, Grad!* The quilt top design would make a beautiful Mother's Day gift, or perhaps a gift for someone recovering from an illness. But really these flower patterns could grow just about anywhere. They could even be border elements in any quilt you like.

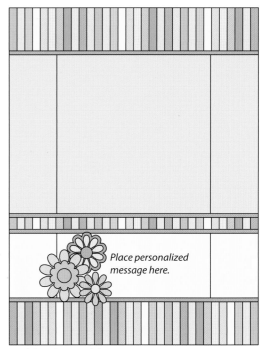

Place personalized message here.

Quilt back assembly

Celtic Knot

Celebrate his (or her!) birthday in style with this clean, modern design.

QUILT TOP MATERIALS

- Block fabrics: 12 different fat quarters
- Background fabric: 3 yards
- Binding fabric: ⅝ yard
- Batting: 68″ × 85″

QUILT TOP CUTTING INSTRUCTIONS

Note

You will make 4 piles of fabric while cutting the block fabrics. See the block assembly diagram (page 37).

- Pile A will form the centers of the blocks.
- Pile B will form the inner borders of the blocks.
- Pile C will form the outer borders of the blocks.
- Pile D will form the outer little squares in the corner of each block.

Cutting continues (page 37)

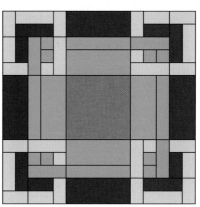

Celtic Knot block

FINISHED QUILT: 57½″ × 74½″
FINISHED BLOCKS: 15″ × 15″

Fabrics shown are from the Legacy collection by Angela Walters for Art Gallery Fabrics and Kona cotton by Robert Kaufman Fabrics.

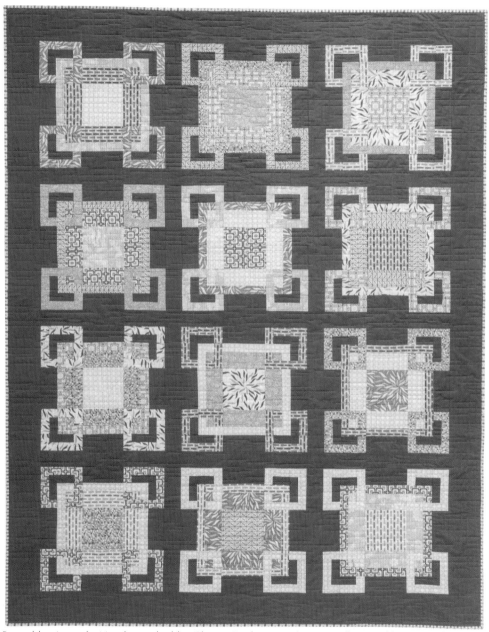

Pieced by Amanda Murphy; quilted by Cherry Guidry using Squares All Around by Sweet Dreams Quilt Studio

CUTTING INSTRUCTIONS CONTINUED

From *each* fat quarter of block fabric:

Refer to the cutting chart (at right) to cut the following pieces in the most efficient manner.

- Cut 1 strip 5½" × 18".

  Subcut a square 5½" × 5½". Place it in pile A.

  Subcut the remainder of the 5½" strip into 2 rectangles 2½" × 12". Place these in pile B.

- Cut 9 strips 1½" × 18".

  Subcut the first strip into 2 rectangles 1½" × 7". Place 1 in pile B and 1 in pile C.

  Subcut the next 3 strips into 2 rectangles 1½" × 12" and 4 rectangles 1½" × 3½". Place all of these in pile C.

  Place a full 1½" × 18" strip in pile D.

  Subcut the remaining strips into 1 rectangle 1½" × 10½", 1 rectangle 1½" × 7", 4 rectangles 1½" × 3½" and 12 rectangles 1½" × 2½". Place all of these in pile D.

From the background fabric:

- Cut 12 strips 1½" × WOF. Subcut into 12 rectangles 1½" × 18" and 12 rectangles 1½" × 10½". Set these aside for piecing the blocks.

- Cut 16 strips 2½" × WOF.

  Subcut 8 of these strips into 24 rectangles 2½" × 12". Set these aside for piecing the blocks.

  Subcut 4 of the remaining strips into 8 rectangles 2½" × 15½". From remaining 4 strips, piece 3 rectangles 2½" × 49½". Set these aside for sashing.

- Cut 7 strips 4½" × WOF. Piece 2 rectangles 4½" × 49½" for the top and bottom borders. Piece 2 rectangles 4½" × 74½" for the side borders.

From the binding fabric:

- Cut 8 strips 2¼" × WOF.

WOF = width of fabric

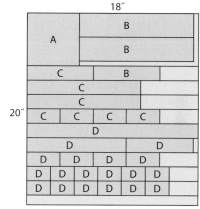

Cutting chart

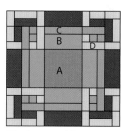

Block assembly

Unless otherwise noted, press seams open.

1. Take a 5½″ × 5½″ square from pile A. Take a different set of prints from pile B, a third set of prints from pile C, and a fourth set of prints from pile D. Repeat until you have 12 different groupings of fabrics with a set of A, B, C, and D prints in each.

Work on 1 block at a time.

2. Join a B rectangle 2½″ × 12″, a C rectangle 1½″ × 12″, and a background rectangle 2½″ × 12″. Press the seams toward the center fabric. Repeat to make a second strip set. Subcut the strip sets into 2 units each 5½″ wide (4 total). **Figure 1**

3. Join the C, B, and D rectangles (each 1½″ × 7″) as shown. Press the seams toward the center B strip. Subcut the strip set into 4 units 1½″ wide. **Figure 2**

4. Join a C rectangle 1½″ × 3½″ and a D rectangle 1½″ × 3½″ to either side of these units, as shown. Repeat to make 4 units total. **Figure 3**

5. Join a D rectangle 1½″ × 18″ to a background rectangle 1½″ × 18″. Join a D rectangle 1½″ × 10½″ to a background rectangle 1½″ × 10½″. From the strip sets, cut 4 units 3½″ wide and 4 units 2½″ wide. **Figure 4**

6. Join a D rectangle 1½″ × 2½″ onto each side of a 3½″ strip-set unit and to a single side of a 2½″ strip-set unit, as shown. Repeat this step to make 4 of each. **Figure 5**

7. Join the units from Steps 3–5, as shown. **Figure 6**

8. Arrange 4 corner units, 4 matching C/B/D units, and the 5½″ × 5½″ A square from as shown, rotating the corner units as needed to create the woven knot design. Join the blocks into rows, pressing the seams toward the outside and center squares. Join the rows. **Figures 7 and 8**

9. Repeat Steps 2–8 to complete a total of 12 blocks.

1
B
C
Background

2
C
B
D

3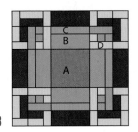
Make 4.

4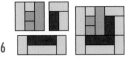
Background
D

5
Make 4 of each.

6
Make 4.

7

8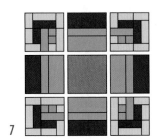
C
B
D
A

Quilt Top Assembly

1. Join 3 blocks to 2 background rectangles 2½″ × 15½″ to form a row. Repeat to make a total of 4 rows of 3 blocks each.

2. Join 4 block rows with 3 background rectangles 2½″ × 49½″.

3. Join a background rectangle 4½″ × 49½″ to the top and bottom of the quilt top.

4. Join a background rectangle 4½″ × 74½″ to each side of the quilt top.

Quilt top assembly

67½″ × 84½″ unfinished
(5″ larger on all sides than
the quilt top)

Make a bold statement
with this larger-than-life-size
block for the back of the quilt!

QUILT BACK MATERIALS

- Block center fabric: 1 fat quarter of a solid or blender
- Block inner border fabric: ⅝ yard
- Block outer border fabric: ½ yard
- Block square corners fabric: ¾ yard
- Appliquéd numbers fabric: 1 fat eighth of a solid or blender
- Background fabric: 3½ yards
- Appliqué thread, 28 weight: in coordinating colors

- Paper-backed fusible web: ½ yard 18″ wide
- Tear-away stabilizer: ½ yard 18″ wide, or 1 sheet* 15″ × 24″
- Tools for personalization (pages 8–10)

If you don't have larger sheets of stabilizer on hand, you can use smaller sheets and overlap them a bit so that they back the entire appliqué area. If you prefer not to use stabilizer, you can heavily starch the background fabric.

QUILT BACK CUTTING INSTRUCTIONS

From the block center (A) fabric:

- Cut 1 square 16″ × 16″.

From the block inner border (B) fabric:

- Cut 2 strips 6½″ × WOF.

- Cut 1 strip 3½″ × WOF.

From the block outer border (C) fabric:

- Cut 4 strips 3½″ × WOF. Set aside 3 strips. Subcut the remaining strip into 4 rectangles 3½″ × 9½″.

From the block square corners (D) fabric:

- Cut 6 strips 3½″ × WOF. Set aside 3 strips. Subcut the remaining strips into 12 rectangles 3½″ × 6½″ and 4 rectangles 3½″ × 9½″.

From the background fabric:

- Cut a 67½″ length from your background fabric. Turn the strip lengthwise and subcut into 1 rectangle 14″ × 67½″ and 1 rectangle 26″ × 67½″.

- From the remaining background fabric:

  Cut 3 strips 11½″ × WOF. Piece 2 rectangles 11½″ × 45½″.

  Cut 2 strips 6½″ × WOF.

  Cut 2 strips 3½″ × WOF·

WOF = width of fabric

> **Note**
>
> This quilt back is pieced vertically because of the big block in the center. If you prefer the seams to hang horizontally, or you are using a directional print, you might want to increase your background yardage and alter the manner in which you cut the fabric.

Personalization

1. Following the instructions in Appliqué Basics (page 104), choose numbers (pullout page P1) to commemorate the day or the recipient's age and trace those large numbers on the back of the paper-backed fusible web, if desired. Fuse the rough side of the fusible web to wrong side of the numbers fabric. Cut out the numbers.

2. Fuse the numbers to the block center A square 16″ × 16″.

3. Refer to Tips and Techniques (page 104) to back the block with tear-away stabilizer and, using 28-weight thread, appliqué using the blanket stitch around the fused numbers.

4. Trim the block center square to 15½″ × 15½″.

5. If desired, refer to Personalizing Your Quilts (page 7) to add your unique message using the method of your choice. Refer to the quilt assembly diagram (page 43) to place and apply the message to the quilt back. *Remember to place text at least ¼″ from all outer edges so it will not be lost in the seam allowances.* For this quilt I used Lesley Riley's TAP Transfer Artist Paper to write *Happy Birthday* across the background 26″ × 67½″ rectangle, about 6″ down from the wide upper edge.

Quilt Back Block Assembly

Hint

Refer to the illustrations for making the smaller blocks on the quilt top (page 38) as needed while completing Steps 1–7.

1. Join an inner border B strip 6½″ × WOF and a background strip 6½″ × WOF to either side of an outer border C strip 3½″ × WOF. Press the seams toward the center strip. Repeat to make another strip set. Subcut the strip sets into 4 units 15½″ wide.

2. Join an outer border C strip and a square corner D strip to either side of an inner border B strip, each 3½″ × WOF. Subcut the strip set into 4 units 3½″ wide.

3. Join a C rectangle 3½″ × 9½″ and a D rectangle 3½″ × 9½″ to either side of these units, as shown. Press the seams toward the center. Repeat this step to make 4 corner units. Figure 9

9

4. Join a D strip 3½″ × WOF to a background strip 3½″ × WOF. Repeat to make another strip set. From the strip sets, cut 4 units 6½″ wide and 4 units 9½″ wide. Figure 10

10 Background
D

5. Join a 3½″ × 6½″ D rectangle to each side of the 9½″ unit and a single side of the 6½″ unit from the previous step, as shown in Quilt Block Assembly, Step 6. Repeat this step to make 4 of each.

6. Join the units from Steps 3–5 as in Quilt Block Assembly, Step 7, pressing the seams toward the rectangular units. Make 4 of each corner unit.

7. Arrange the quilt block. Join the blocks into rows, pressing the seams toward the outside and center squares. Join the rows.

Quilt Back Assembly

1. Join a background rectangle 11½″ × 45½″ to each side of the block.

2. Join a background rectangle 14″ × 67½″ to the top of the quilt top.

3. Join a background rectangle 26″ × 67½″ to the bottom of the quilt top. Make sure to orient the writing so that it is right side up!

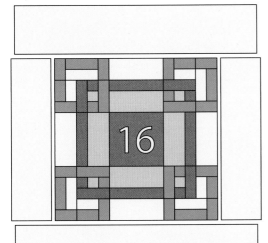

Place personalized message here.

Quilt back assembly

Finishing

Refer to Finishing Basics (page 108) for more detailed instructions.

1. Layer the backing, batting, and quilt top. Quilt as desired.

2. Join the 2¼″ × WOF binding strips into 1 continuous piece for binding. Press, folding the strip in half lengthwise. Sew the binding to the quilt using your preferred method.

Change It Up

The *Celtic Knot* quilt is very versatile. It could easily commemorate a first job or a big move (either into one's own place or across the country). It's also one of several quilt designs in this book that could commemorate a special friendship.

Blessings

Commemorate a baptism, first communion, or confirmation with this modern cross design. For a boy's quilt, or just a different look, mix and match these borders with the Celebration Circles border (page 60) or the *Mazel Tov* border (page 56).

QUILT TOP MATERIALS

- Cross and butterfly fabrics: ½ yard each of 6 prints
- Background fabric: 1¼ yards
- Inner border fabric: ¼ yard
- Outer border background fabric: 1¾ yards
- Border cornerstone fabric: ½ yard
- Binding fabric: ½ yard
- Batting: 65″ × 82″
- Appliqué thread, 28 weight: in coordinating colors
- Paper-backed fusible web: 5 yards 18″ wide
- Tear-away stabilizer: 5½ yards 18″ wide, or 9 sheets* 15″ × 24″

If you don't have larger sheets of stabilizer on hand, you can use smaller sheets and overlap them a bit so that they back the entire appliqué area. If you prefer not to use stabilizer, you can heavily starch the background fabric.

QUILT TOP CUTTING INSTRUCTIONS

From the background fabric:

- Cut 2 strips 3½″ × WOF. Subcut into 2 rectangles 3½″ × 36½″.
- Cut 2 strips 6½″ × WOF. Subcut into 2 rectangles 6½″ × 39½″.
- Cut 2 strips 9½″ × WOF. Subcut *each* into a 9½″ × 9½″ square and a 9½″ × 24½″ rectangle.

From the inner border fabric:

- Cut 5 strips 1½″ × WOF. Subcut into 2 rectangles 1½″ × 38½″ and piece the remaining strips into 2 rectangles 1½″ × 45½″.

From the outer border fabric:

- Cut 1 strip 15″ × WOF. Subcut into 1 rectangle 15″ × 40″ for the bottom border.
- Cut 1 strip 11″ × WOF. Subcut into 1 rectangle 11″ × 40″ for the top border.
- From the remaining fabric, cut 1 strip 25″ × WOF. Turn the strip lengthwise and cut 4 strips 9″ × 25″. Piece 2 rectangles 9″ × 49½″ for the side borders. Treat the remaining border fabric as a cross fabric print and cut it according to the directions (page 47).

WOF = width of fabric

Cutting continues (page 47)

FINISHED QUILT: 54½″ × 71½″

Pieced and quilted by Amanda Murphy

CUTTING INSTRUCTIONS CONTINUED

From *each* of the cross fabrics and the remainder of the outer border print:

- Cut 1 strip 3½″ × WOF. Subcut into 7 squares 3½″ × 3½″ (you will have extra). Trim the remainder of the strip to 2″ and then cut 2 squares 2″ × 2″.

- Cut 1 strip 2″ × WOF. Set this aside to use for the Cross block on the back of the quilt.

- Set aside the remainder of the fabric to use for the butterfly appliqué.

From the border cornerstone fabric:

- Cut 1 strip 14½″ × WOF. Subcut into 2 rectangles 14½″ × 8½″. Trim the remaining strip down to 10½″ and then cut 2 rectangles 10½″ × 8½″.

From the binding fabric:

- Cut 7 strips 2¼″ × WOF.

Cross Assembly

1. Draw a diagonal line on the back of each 2″ × 2″ cross square.

2. Lay a 2″ × 2″ cross square on 2 opposite corners of each background 9½″ × 9½″ square, right sides together. Stitch a hairline away from the line, on the side closer to the corner. Trim the seams to ¼″ and press open. **Figure 1**

3. Lay a 2″ × 2″ cross square on 2 opposite corners of each background 9½″ × 24½″ rectangle, right sides together. Stitch a hairline away from the line, on the side closer to the corner. Trim the seams to ¼″ and press open. **Figure 2**

4. Arrange the 3½″ × 3½″ cross squares to form a cross. Join 3 rows of 2 blocks each for the top portion of the cross, 2 rows of 8 blocks each for the middle of the cross, and 8 rows of 2 blocks each for the bottom of the cross. Press seams in opposite directions for each row. (To ensure accurate piecing, press seams of adjoining rows in opposite directions.) **Figure 3**

5. Lay out the pieced cross and background units in rows as shown. Join the units into rows. Join the rows to complete the block. **Figure 4**

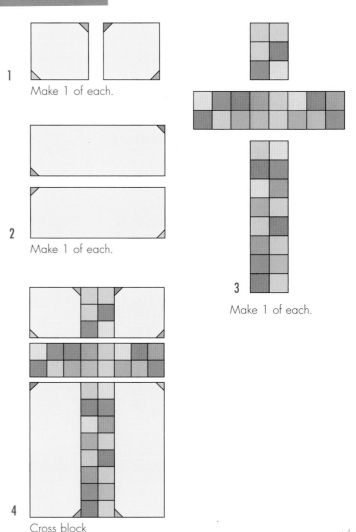

1 Make 1 of each.

2 Make 1 of each.

3 Make 1 of each.

4 Cross block

Borders

1. Trace 23–25 butterfly bodies and wings (pullout page P1) onto the smooth side of the paper-backed fusible web, following the steps shown in the Appliqué Basics (page 104) and using the windowing technique (page 105), if desired.

2. Fuse the rough side of the fusible shapes onto the wrong side of the butterfly fabrics. Cut out the shapes on the traced lines.

3. Remove the paper and arrange the butterflies on the border strips. When you are happy with the arrangement, fuse the butterflies to the border strips to secure them. Use an appliqué pressing sheet or Silicone Release Paper (from C&T Publishing) to keep any fusible residue from overhanging shapes off of your ironing board. Trim the appliqué shapes flush with the borders. Figure 5

4. Refer to Tips and Techniques (page 104) to back the borders with tear-away stabilizer and, using a blanket stitch and 28 weight thread, secure the edges of the appliqué.

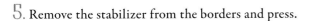

5. Remove the stabilizer from the borders and press.

6. Trim the outer top border to 10½″ × 38½″.

7. Trim the outer bottom border to 14½″ × 38½″.

8. Trim the outer side borders to 8½″ × 47½″.

9. Join a cornerstone rectangle 8½″ × 10½″ to each side of the top border, pressing the seams toward the cornerstones.

10. Join a cornerstone rectangle 8½″ × 14½″ to each side of the bottom border, pressing the seams toward the cornerstones.

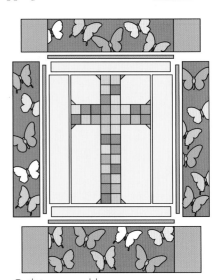

Quilt top assembly

Quilt Top Assembly

1. Join a background rectangle 6½″ × 39½″ to each side of the Cross block.

2. Join a background rectangle 3½″ × 36½″ to the top and bottom of the quilt top.

3. Join an inner border rectangle 1½″ × 45½″ to the sides of the quilt top.

4. Join an inner border rectangle 1½″ × 38½″ to the top and bottom of the quilt top.

5. Join the outer borders to the sides of the quilt top.

6. Join the top and bottom borders to the top and bottom of quilt top.

QUILT BACK

65″ × 81½″ (5″ larger on the top and bottom and a little more than 5″ larger on the sides than the quilt top)

Personalize your gift by adding the recipient's name and the date of their special event on the back.

QUILT BACK MATERIALS

- 2″ Cross block strips set aside while making the quilt top
- Background fabric: 3½ yards
- Top stripe fabric: ⅞ yard
- Middle stripe fabric: ⅓ yard
- Bottom stripe fabric: ¾ yard

QUILT BACK CUTTING INSTRUCTIONS

From *each of the cross strips 2″ × WOF*:

- Cut each strip into 7 squares 2″ × 2″. Trim the remainder of the strip to 1¼″ and then cut 2 squares 1¼″ × 1¼″.

From *the background fabric*:

- Cut 2 strips 20¾″ × WOF. Subcut into 1 rectangle 20¾″ × 40″ and 2 rectangles 20¾″ × 13″. Join the smaller rectangles onto the sides of the larger rectangle to yield a pieced rectangle 20¾″ × 65″.

- Cut 2 strips 13¾″ × WOF. Subcut into 1 rectangle 13¾″ × 40″ and 2 rectangles 13¾″ × 13″. Join the smaller rectangles to each side of the larger rectangle to yield a pieced rectangle 13¾″ × 65″.

- Cut 2 strips 20″ × WOF. Subcut into 1 rectangle 20″ × 37″ and 1 rectangle 20″ × 16½″.

- Cut 1 strip 5″ × WOF. Subcut into 2 squares 5″ × 5″ and 2 rectangles 5″ × 12½″.

Cutting continues (page 50)

CUTTING INSTRUCTIONS CONTINUED

From the top stripe fabric:

- Cut 2 strips 13¼″ × WOF. Subcut into 1 rectangle 13¼″ × 40″ and 2 rectangles 13¼ ½″ × 13″. Join the smaller rectangles to each side of the larger rectangle to yield a pieced rectangle 13¼″ × 65″.

From the middle stripe fabric:

- Cut 2 strips 4¾″ × WOF. Subcut into 1 rectangle 4¾″ × 40″ and 2 rectangles 4¾″ × 13″. Join the smaller rectangles to each side of the larger rectangle to yield a pieced rectangle 4¾″ × 65″.

From the bottom stripe fabric:

- Cut 2 strips 11½″ × WOF. Subcut into 1 rectangle 11½″ × 40″ and 2 rectangles 11½″ × 13″. Join the smaller rectangles to each side of the larger rectangle to yield a pieced rectangle 11½″ × 65″.

WOF = width of fabric

Cross

Make a smaller version of the Cross block (Cross Assembly, page 47) using the 2″ × 2″ and 1¼″ × 1¼″ cross squares, the 5″ × 5″ background squares, and the 5″ × 12½″ rectangles.

Personalization

Refer to Personalizing Your Quilts (page 7) to add your unique message to the quilt back using the method of your choice. You could record the name of the recipient along with the date of the event. *Remember to place text at least ¼″ from all outer edges so it will not be lost in the seam allowances.*

Following the quilt back assembly diagram, transfer the name and date type onto the 20″ × 37″ background rectangle. Make sure that the text starts at least 2″ from the left raw edge and at least ½″ from the bottom edge of the rectangle.

Quilt Back Assembly

1. Join the personalized 20″ × 37″ background rectangle to the right side of the Cross block.

2. Join the 20″ × 16½″ background rectangle to the left side of the Cross block.

3. Lay out the stripe, background, and cross rows, following the quilt back assembly diagram.

4. Join the rows.

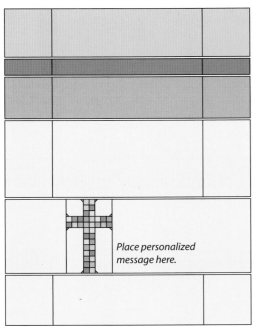

Place personalized message here.

Quilt back assembly

Finishing

Refer to Finishing Basics (page 108) for more detailed instructions.

1. Layer the backing, batting, and quilt top. Quilt as desired.

2. Join the 2¼″ × WOF binding strips into 1 continuous piece for binding. Press, folding the strip in half lengthwise. Sew the binding to the quilt using your preferred method.

Change It Up

You can change the colors on this one if it's for a boy (or maybe even a tomboy!). This quilt is perfect for christenings, first communions, baptisms, and confirmations. But a graduate of a parochial school or someone stepping into professional ministry would wrap up comfortably in this one, too.

Mazel Tov

Celebrate a Bat Mitzvah or Bar Mitzvah with a design that highlights the Star of David in a modern way.

QUILT TOP MATERIALS

- Star of David fabrics: 1 fat quarter each of 8 prints
- Background fabric: 1½ yards
- Inner border fabric: ¼ yard
- Outer border fabric: 1¾ yards
- Border cornerstones fabric: ½ yard
- Main border accent fabric: 1 yard
- Other border accent fabrics: 1 yard each of 2 fabrics
- Binding fabric: ½ yard
- Batting: 65″ × 87″
- Appliqué thread, 28 weight: a color matching the main border accent
- Appliqué thread, 50 weight: a color matching the other border accents
- Paper-backed fusible web: 2½ yards 18″ wide
- Lite Steam-A-Seam 2 fusible tape, ½″ wide and ¼″ wide: 16 yards each
- Tear-away stabilizer: 5½ yards 18″ wide, or 9 sheets* 15″ × 24″
- Clover fusible or regular bias tape makers: ¾″ (18 mm) and ½″ (12 mm) sizes (*optional*)
- 60° triangle ruler (*optional*)

* If you don't have larger sheets of stabilizer on hand, you can use smaller sheets and overlap them a bit so that they back the entire appliqué area. If you prefer not to use stabilizer, you can heavily starch the background fabric.

QUILT TOP CUTTING INSTRUCTIONS

From *each* of the Star of David prints:

- Cut 2 strips 4½″ wide, orienting the fat quarter in any way you choose. Subcut into 6 triangles per fabric, using the Large Triangle Pattern (page 61) or a 60° triangle ruler. (Align the ruler on top of the template first to ensure you're cutting along the correct lines!)

- Cut 1 strip 2½″ wide and set it aside for the smaller Star of David on the quilt back.

From the background fabric:

- Cut 1 strip 7½″ × WOF. Subcut into 1 rectangle 7½″ × 36½″.

- Cut 1 strip 6½″ × WOF. Subcut into 1 rectangle 6½″ × 36½″.

- Cut 4 strips 4½″ × WOF. Subcut into 56 triangles using the Large Triangle Pattern (page 61) or a 60° triangle ruler.

- Cut 2 strips 5″ × WOF from the remaining fabric. Subcut into 2 rectangles 5″ × 32½″.

Cutting continues (page 55)

Note

If you are using a directional print, cut 5″-wide strips lengthwise and piece these rectangles so that the print runs up and down the length of the side border pieces.

FINISHED QUILT: 54½″ × 71½″

Fabrics shown are from the Botanics and Architextures collections by Carolyn Friedlander for Robert Kaufman Fabrics.

Pieced and quilted by Amanda Murphy

CUTTING INSTRUCTIONS CONTINUED

From the inner border fabric:

- Cut 5 strips 1½″ × WOF. Subcut into 2 rectangles 1½″ × 38½″ and piece the remaining strips into 2 rectangles 1½″ × 45½″.

From the outer border fabric:

- Cut 1 strip 15″ × WOF. Subcut into 1 rectangle 15″ × 40″ for the bottom border.

- Cut 1 strip 11″ × WOF. Subcut into 1 rectangle 11″ × 40″ for the top border.

- From the remaining fabric, cut 1 strip 25″ × WOF. Turn the strip lengthwise and cut 4 strips 9″ × 25″. Piece into 2 rectangles 9″ × 49½″ for the side borders.

WOF = width of fabric

From the border cornerstone fabric:

- Cut 1 strip 14½″ × WOF. Subcut into 2 rectangles 14½″ × 8½″. Trim the remaining strip down to 10½″ and then cut 2 rectangles 10½″ × 8½″.

From the binding fabric:

- Cut 7 strips 2¼″ × WOF.

From the main border accent fabric:

- Cut 1 strip 15″ × WOF and 1 strip 9″ × WOF from your favorite print.

From *each* of the other 2 border accent fabrics:

- Cut 2 strips 13″ × WOF. Subcut a single print into 24–30 additional 1⅜″-wide strips *on the bias*. Subcut the other print into 24–30 additional ⅞″-wide strips *on the bias*.

Star of David Assembly

1. Arrange the large background and star triangles in rows to form a Star of David as shown in the block assembly diagram (below).

2. Sew pairs of triangles together. Press all the seams in what will be the first row in the same direction, and press each adjoining row in opposite directions. **Figure 1**

3. Join the pairs of triangles together in rows. (To correctly join the rows, you will need to align the seamline as shown in Figure 3, rather than aligning the points of the triangles.) Press as in Step 2. **Figures 2–4**

4. Join the rows.

5. Trim the block sides so that the star points are ¼″ from the raw edge of the block.

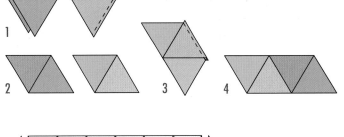

Star of David block

Borders

1. Back the 15″ × WOF and 9″ × WOF border accent strips with paper-backed fusible web. Using your rotary cutter, subcut a total of 24–30 wavy strips 1¼″–3″ wide. Figure 5

2. Use the bias tape maker or an iron to fold and press the 1⅜″-wide border accent bias strips into ¾″-wide bias tape. Back the bias tape with ½″-wide fusible tape. Figures 6 & 7

3. Use the bias tape maker or an iron to fold and press the ⅞″-wide border accent bias strips into ½″-wide bias tape. Back the bias tape with ¼″-wide fusible tape.

4. Remove the paper backing from the wavy strips and place them randomly along the 11″ × 40″, 15″ × 40″, and 9″ × 49½″ border rectangles, following the quilt top assembly diagram. Leave room between them for the bias tape. (Don't worry if the wavy strips are wider than the background fabric; you will trim everything later.) Following the manufacturer's instructions, fuse the wavy strips in place.

5. Refer to Tips and Techniques (page 104) to back the borders with tear-away stabilizer and, using a blanket stitch and 28 weight thread, appliqué the wavy strips in place to secure.

6. Remove the paper backing from the bias tape strips and apply them to the border rectangles, following the quilt top assembly diagram. Fuse in place.

7. Use an invisible hem stitch in 50-weight thread to secure the bias tape.

8. Remove the stabilizer from the borders and press, using an appliqué pressing sheet or Silicone Release Paper (from C&T Publishing) to protect your ironing board from fusible residue.

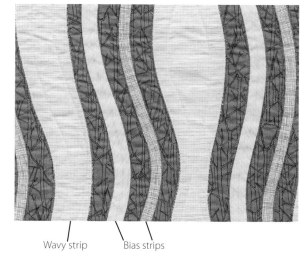

5

Wavy strip   Bias strips

Border detail

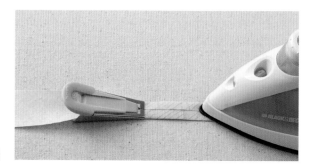

6

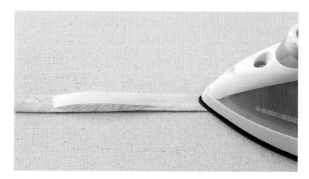

7

9. Trim the borders as follows, removing any wavy strips and bias tape strips that extend beyond the edges of the borders.

> **Outer top border:** 10½″ × 38½″
> **Outer bottom border:** 14½″ × 38½″
> **Outer side borders:** 8½″ × 47½″

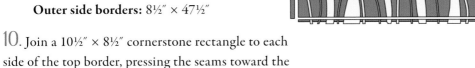

10. Join a 10½″ × 8½″ cornerstone rectangle to each side of the top border, pressing the seams toward the cornerstones.

11. Join a 14½″ × 8½″ cornerstone rectangle to each side of the bottom border, pressing the seams toward the cornerstones.

Quilt Top Assembly

1. Join a background rectangle 5″ × 32½″ to each side of the Star of David block. Trim the block if needed to 36½″ wide.

2. Join the background rectangle 6½″ × 36½″ to the top of the quilt top.

3. Join the background rectangle 7½″ × 36½″ to the bottom of the quilt top.

4. Join an inner border rectangle 1½″ × 45½″ to the sides of the quilt top.

5. Join an inner border rectangle 1½″ × 38½″ to the top and bottom of the quilt top.

6. Join the outer borders to the sides of the quilt top.

7. Join the top and bottom border to the top and bottom of the quilt top.

Quilt top assembly

QUILT BACK

65″ × 81½″ unfinished
(5″ larger on the top and bottom and a little more than 5″ larger on the sides than the quilt top)

Personalize your gift by adding the recipient's name and the date of their Bar or Bat Mitzvah on the back. Or, leave it simple with just a star!

QUILT BACK MATERIALS

- Star strips 2½″ wide set aside from the quilt top
- Background fabric: 3½ yards
- Top stripe fabric: ⅞ yard
- Middle stripe fabric: ⅓ yard
- Bottom stripe fabric: ¾ yard
- 60° triangle ruler (*optional*)

QUILT BACK CUTTING INSTRUCTIONS

From *each* of the 2½″-wide star strips:

- Subcut each strip into 6 triangles using the Small Triangle Pattern (page 61) or a 60° triangle ruler. (Align the ruler on top of the template first to ensure you're cutting along the correct lines!)

From the background fabric:

- Cut 2 strips 24¼″ × WOF. Subcut into 1 rectangle 24¼″ × 40″ and 2 rectangles 24¼″ × 13″. Join the smaller rectangles to each side of the larger rectangle to yield a rectangle 24¼″ × 65″.

- Cut 2 strips 13¾″ × WOF. Subcut into 1 rectangle 13¾″ × 40″ and 2 rectangles 13¾″ × 13″. Join the smaller rectangles to each side of the larger rectangle to yield a rectangle 13¾″ × 65″.

CUTTING INSTRUCTIONS CONTINUED

- Cut 2 strips 16½″ × WOF. Subcut into 1 rectangle 16½″ × 37″ and 1 rectangle 16½″ × 15″.

- Cut 3 strips 2½″ × WOF. Subcut into 56 triangles using the Small Triangle Pattern (page 61) or a 60° triangle ruler.

From the top stripe fabric:

- Cut 2 strips 13¼″ × WOF. Subcut into 1 rectangle 13¼″ × 40″ and 2 rectangles 13¼ × 13″. Join the smaller rectangles to each side of the larger rectangle to yield 1 rectangle 13¼″ × 65″.

From the middle stripe fabric:

- Cut 2 strips 4¾″ × WOF. Subcut into 1 rectangle 4¾″ × 40″ and 2 rectangles 4¾″ × 13″. Join the smaller rectangles to each side of the larger rectangle to yield 1 rectangle 4¾″ × 65″.

From the bottom stripe fabric:

- Cut 2 strips 11½″ × WOF. Subcut into 1 rectangle 11½″ × 40″ and 2 rectangles 11½″ × 13″. Join the smaller rectangles to each side of the larger rectangle to yield 1 rectangle 11½″ × 65″.

WOF = width of fabric

Star of David

Refer to Star of David Assembly (page 55) for the quilt top to make a smaller version of the block using the small triangles.

Personalization

Refer to Personalizing Your Quilts (page 7) to add your unique message to the quilt back using the method of your choice. You could record the name of the recipient along with the date of the event. *Remember to place text at least ¼″ from all outer edges so it will not be lost in the seam allowances.* You may want to wait until the quilt back is assembled to choose the best placement for your message.

Quilt Back Assembly

1. Join the 16½″ × 37″ background rectangle to the right side of the Star of David block.

2. Join the 16½″ × 15″ background rectangle to the left side of the Star of David block.

3. Trim the Star of David row to 65″ wide.

4. Lay out the background, stripe, and Star of David rows, following the quilt back assembly diagram (at right).

5. Join the rows.

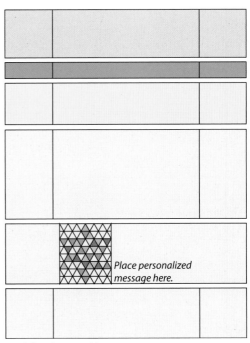

Place personalized message here.

Quilt back assembly

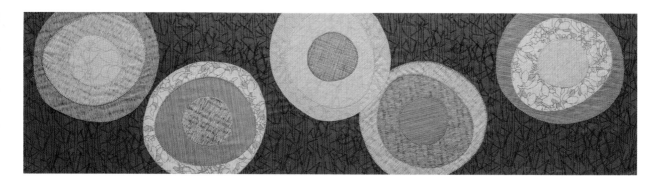

CELEBRATION CIRCLES BORDER

You will need the following in addition to the materials listed in Quilt Top Materials (page 52).

BORDER MATERIALS

- Border rectangles as specified in *Mazel Tov* Quilt Top Cutting Instructions (page 55)

- Fat quarters of a few additional fabrics to add variety

- Appliqué thread, 28 weight: a variety of colors to match additional appliqué fabrics

- Paper-backed fusible web, 18″ wide: 1 additional yard

BORDER ASSEMBLY

1. Follow the steps shown in Appliqué Basics (page 104). Using the Celebration Circles patterns (pullout page P2) or drawing freehand, trace 22–24 sets of wonky circle shapes onto the paper-backed fusible web, one circle inside another.

2. Cut the shapes apart and cut the excess fusible from within each shape, leaving about ¼″ of fusible web on the inside edge of each circle.

3. Fuse the circles to the wrong side of a variety of fabrics, and then cut out the shapes on the traced lines.

4. Remove the paper and arrange the shapes as desired on the border rectangles. Fuse the shapes to secure them. Use an appliqué pressing sheet or Silicone Release Paper (from C&T Publishing) under any circles that extend beyond the edge of the background fabric to protect your ironing board from fusible residue.

5. Refer to Tips and Techniques (page 104) to back the fabric with the tear-away stabilizer and, using a blanket stitch and 28 weight thread, secure the appliqués.

6. Bring the threads to the back and knot them. Clip the threads, leaving ½″ tails.

7. Remove the stabilizer.

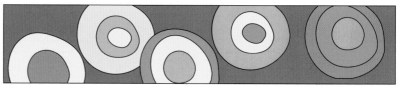

Alternate option: Celebration Circles Border

Refer to Finishing Basics (page 108) for more detailed instructions.

1. Layer the backing, batting, and quilt top. Quilt as desired.

2. Join the 2¼″ × WOF binding strips into 1 continuous piece for binding. Press, folding the strip in half lengthwise. Sew the binding to the quilt using your preferred method.

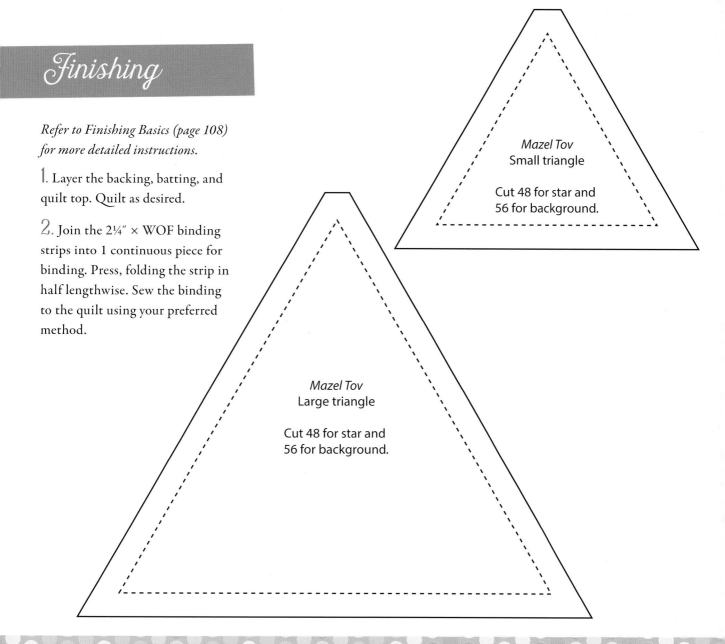

Mazel Tov
Small triangle

Cut 48 for star and 56 for background.

Mazel Tov
Large triangle

Cut 48 for star and 56 for background.

Change It Up

Use an alternative border design, such as Celebration Circles (previous page), to change the look of this quilt. If you love the scale of the big, appliquéd butterflies on the *Blessings* quilt (page 44) but want a less feminine look, then try this design. The Celebration Circles border design, the border design pictured in the *Mazel Tov* quilt (page 52), and the border design on the *Blessings* quilt (page 44) can all be easily interchanged!

Congratulations, Grad!

Perfect for a dorm room or first apartment, this twin-size quilt is sure to please any grad. Choose a background with dynamic contrast to make the center star pop!

QUILT TOP MATERIALS

Star fabrics:

You will need 7 star fabrics. All 7 fabrics are used for the central star, with fabric 1 being the star points, fabric 4 being the most used, and fabric 7 being the star center. (I also used fabric 7 for the side border triangles.) For the star points on the border of the quilt, you will use only fabrics 1–5.

- Star fabric 1: ⅜ yard
- Star fabric 2: ⅝ yard
- Star fabric 3: 1 yard
- Star fabric 4: ⅞ yard
- Star fabric 5: ½ yard
- Star fabric 6: ¼ yard
- Star fabric 7: ¼ yard
- Star background fabric: 2⅔ yards

Note

I recommend heavily starching all the fabrics you are working with, especially the fabrics for the star points and the triangle blocks that are joined to them, to avoid stretching the bias edges when making a Lone Star quilt.

Other materials

- General background fabric: 1¾ yards
- Narrow border fabric: ¼ yard (I used star fabric 1.)
- Wide border fabric: ¼ yard (I used star fabric 4.)
- Side border triangle fabric: 1 yard (I used star fabric 7.)
- Binding fabric: ¾ yard
- Batting: 85″ × 107″
- Spray starch or spray starch alternative (I prefer Mary Ellen's Best Press.)

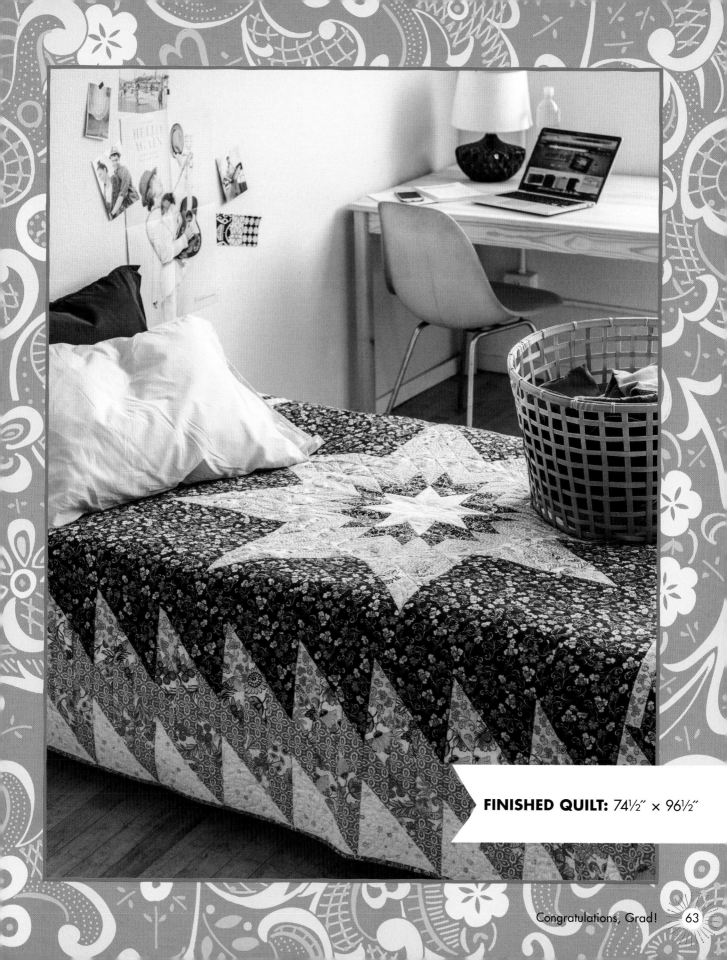

FINISHED QUILT: 74½″ × 96½″

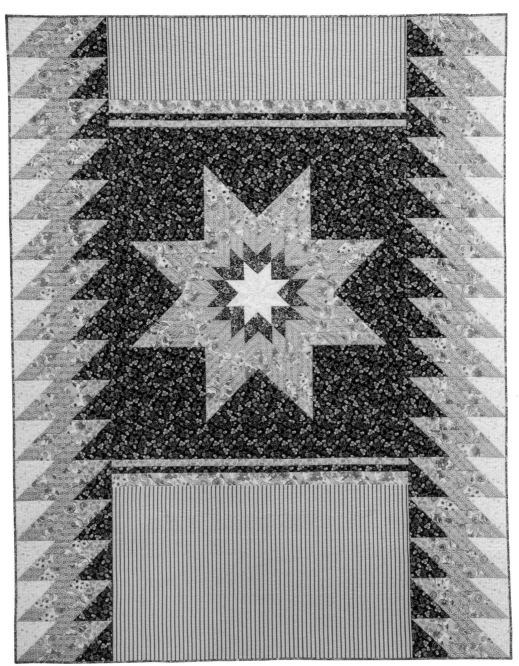

Pieced and quilted by Amanda Murphy

QUILT TOP CUTTING INSTRUCTIONS

Note: Triangles are cut oversized and will be trimmed later.

From star fabric 1:

Cut 4 strips 2½″ × WOF.

From star fabric 2:

Cut 8 strips 2½″ × WOF.

From star fabric 3:

Cut 12 strips 2½″ × WOF.

From star fabric 4:

Cut 10 strips 2½″ × WOF.

From star fabric 5:

Cut 6 strips 2½″ × WOF.

From star fabric 6:

Cut 2 strips 2½″ × WOF.

From star fabric 7:

Cut 1 strip 2½″ × WOF.

From star background fabric:

- Cut 1 strip 9½″ × WOF. Subcut into 4 squares 9½″. Cut each square in half diagonally to yield 8 triangles.

- Cut 2 strips 12¾″ × WOF. Subcut into 4 squares 12¾″ × 12¾″. Cut each square in half diagonally to yield 8 triangles.

- Cut 4 strips 7″ × WOF. Subcut into 16 squares 7″ × 7″. Cut each square in half diagonally to yield 32 triangles.

- Cut 3 strips 6″ × WOF. Piece into 2 rectangles 6″ × 45½″.

- Cut 2 strips 3½″ × WOF. Subcut into 2 rectangle 3½″ × 39½″.

- Cut 3 strips 1½″ × WOF. Piece into 2 rectangles 1½″ × 45½″.

From the general background fabric:

- Cut 2 strips 26½″ × WOF and 1 strip 12½″ × WOF. Piece 1 rectangle 26½″ × 45½″. Trim the remaining 26½″ strip to 12½″ wide and piece 1 rectangle 12½″ × 45½″.

From the narrow border fabric:

- Cut 3 strips 1½″ × WOF. Piece into 2 rectangles 1½″ × 45½″.

From the wide border fabric:

- Cut 3 strips 2½″ × WOF. Piece into 2 rectangles 2½″ × 45½″.

From the side border triangle fabric:

- Cut 4 strips 7″ × WOF. Subcut into 16 squares 7″ × 7″. Cut each square in half diagonally to yield 32 triangles.

From the binding:

- Cut 10 strips 2¼″ × WOF.

WOF = width of fabric

Central Star Block Assembly

1. Make a strip set from the strips of fabrics 1, 2, 3, and 4, offsetting the strips by 2½" as shown. Cut 8 units 2½" wide at a 45° angle from this strip set. **Figure 1**

2. Make a strip set from fabrics 2, 3, 4, and 5, offsetting the strips by 2½" as shown. Cut 8 units 2½" wide at a 45° angle from this strip set. **Figure 2**

3. Make a strip set from fabrics 3, 4, 5, and 6, offsetting the strips by 2½" as shown. Cut 8 units 2½" wide at a 45° angle from this strip set. **Figure 3**

4. Make a strip set from fabrics 4, 5, 6, and 7, offsetting the strips by 2½" as shown. Cut 8 units 2½" wide at a 45° angle from this strip set. **Figure 4**

5. Join 1 unit each from Steps 1, 2, 3, and 4 to form a star point. Pin carefully when doing this—stick a pin at each seam intersection through both units, ¼" from their raw edge, to make sure the diamond points will align when the 2 pieces are joined. **Figure 5**

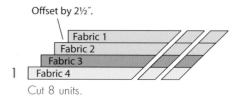

Offset by 2½".

Fabric 1
Fabric 2
Fabric 3
Fabric 4

1 Cut 8 units.

Fabric 2
Fabric 3
Fabric 4
Fabric 5

2 Cut 8 units.

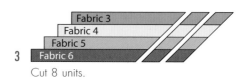

Fabric 3
Fabric 4
Fabric 5
Fabric 6

3 Cut 8 units.

Fabric 4
Fabric 5
Fabric 6
Fabric 7

4 Cut 8 units.

Pin the Lone Star units.

6. Join a 12¾" × 12¾" star background triangle and a 9½" × 9½" star background triangle to each star point, as shown. Make 8 units total, half of which are mirror images of the other half. Be careful not to stretch the bias edges while sewing. **Figure 6**

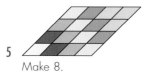

5 Make 8.

6 Make 4 of each.

7. Join a star point and a mirror-image star point together as shown. Repeat this step to make a total of 4 quarter-star units. Figure 7

8. Join the units from Step 7 to form a Lone Star as shown. Trim the Lone Star block to 39½″ × 39½″.

9. Join a 3½″ × 39½″ star background rectangle to each side of the Lone Star block, pressing the seams open.

10. Join a 6″ × 45½″ star background rectangle to the top and bottom of the Lone Star block, pressing the seams open. Figure 8

Side Border Assembly

1. Make 3 strip sets from 1 strip each of fabrics 1, 2, and 3, offsetting the strips by 2½″ as shown. Cut 32 units 2½″ wide at a 45° angle from these strip sets. Figure 9

2. Make 3 strip sets from 1 strip each of fabrics 2, 3, and 4, offsetting the strips by 2½″ as shown. Cut 32 units 2½″ wide at a 45° angle from these strip sets. Figure 10

3. Make 3 strip sets from 1 strip each of fabrics 3, 4, and 5, offsetting the strips by 2½″ as shown. Cut 32 units 2½″ wide at a 45° angle from these strip sets. Figure 11

4. Join 1 unit from each of Steps 1, 2, and 3 to form a border star point. Repeat this step to make a total of 32 border star points. Figure 12

5. Join 1 star background 7″ × 7″ triangle and 1 border 7″ × 7″ triangle to each star point as shown, being careful not to stretch the bias edges. Repeat this step to make 16 blocks and 16 mirror-image blocks. Figure 13

6. Trim each block to 6½″ × 15″. (The star points should be ¼″ in from the raw edges of the fabric.)

7. Following the quilt top assembly diagram (page 68), join 2 sets of 16 blocks together to form the borders.

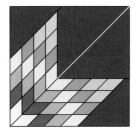

7

Make 4.

8

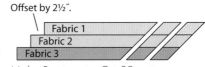

Offset by 2½″.

Fabric 1
Fabric 2
Fabric 3

9

Make 3 strip sets. Cut 32 units.

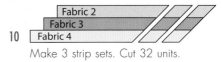

Fabric 2
Fabric 3
Fabric 4

10

Make 3 strip sets. Cut 32 units.

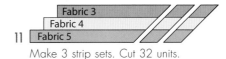

Fabric 3
Fabric 4
Fabric 5

11

Make 3 strip sets. Cut 32 units.

12

Make 32.

13

Make 16 of each.

Quilt Top Assembly

1. Join a 1½" × 45½" narrow border rectangle to the top and bottom of the Lone Star block, pressing the seams toward the borders.

2. Join a 1½" × 45½" star background rectangle to the top and bottom of the Lone Star block, pressing the seams away from the quilt top center.

3. Join a 2½" × 45½" wide border rectangle to the top and bottom of the Lone Star block, pressing the seams toward the borders.

4. Join a 26½" × 45½" general background rectangle to the bottom of the quilt top. Join a 12½" × 45½" general background rectangle to the top of the quilt top.

5. Join a side border to both sides of the quilt top.

Quilt top assembly

84½" × 106½" unfinished
(5" larger on all sides than
the quilt top)

Personalize the back of the
quilt with a special message
or the recipient's name, or
use the center of the star for
a large signature panel for
friends and family (page 70).

QUILT BACK MATERIALS

- Star center fabric: ¾ yard
- Star points fabric: ⅞ yard
- Horizontal band fabric:
  1¼ yards
- Background fabric: 6 yards
- Fabric pens or tools for
  personalization (pages 8–10)
  and tear-away stabilizer
  (if appliquéing or machine
  embroidering)

QUILT BACK CUTTING INSTRUCTIONS

From the star center fabric:

- Cut 1 strip 25" × WOF. Subcut
  into 1 square 25" × 25".

From the star point fabric:

- Cut 2 strips 13" × WOF. Subcut
  into 4 squares 13" × 13".

From the horizontal band fabric:

- Cut 1 strip 13" × WOF. Subcut
  into 2 squares 13" × 13".

- Cut 1 strip 24½" × WOF. Subcut
  into 2 rectangles 24½" × 18½".

From the background fabric:

- Cut 1 strip 30½" × WOF. Turn the
  strip lengthwise and subcut into
  3 rectangles 12½" × 30½".

- Cut 2 lengths of yardage
  84½". Subcut into 1 rectangle
  84½" × 23½" and 1 rectangle
  84½" × 35½". Subcut the remaining
  yardage into 2 squares 13" × 13"
  and 1 more rectangle 12½" × 30½".

WOF = width of fabric

Personalization

1. Refer to Personalizing Your Quilts (page 7) to commemorate the day with a personal message on the star center square. You could also have people sign the star center square, using the writing tips (Handwriting, page 9) and then heat setting the signatures on the panel with an iron. *Remember to place text at least ¼" from all outer edges so it will not be lost in the seam allowances.*

2. Trim the star center square to 24½" × 24½" after personalizing it.

An alternative quilt back design with a signature panel

Half-Square Triangles Assembly

1. Draw a diagonal line on the wrong side of the 13" × 13" background and horizontal band squares.

2. Place a marked square, right sides together, on top of a 13" × 13" star point square and pin. Sew ¼" away from both sides of the drawn line. Repeat with all the remaining 13" background and horizontal band squares.

3. Cut the squares apart on the drawn line to yield 2 half-square triangle units. Press the seams open.

4. Trim the half-square triangle unit to 12½" × 12½".

5. Repeat Steps 2–4 with the remaining squares to yield a total of 8 half-square triangle units. Figure 13

6. Join 2 background half-square triangles together as shown. Repeat with the remaining background half-square triangles. Figure 14

7. Join 2 horizontal band half-square triangles together as shown. Repeat with the remaining horizontal band half-square triangles. Figure 15

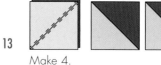

13

Make 4.

14

Make 2.

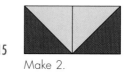

15

Make 2.

Quilt Back Assembly

1. Following the quilt back assembly diagram, join the horizontal band rectangles, the horizontal half-square triangle units, and the star center square together to form a row.

2. Join a 12½″ × 30½″ background rectangle to each side of each background half-square triangle unit to form a row. Repeat with the remaining background rectangles.

3. Join the rows from Step 2 to the top and bottom of the star center row.

4. Join the 23½″ × 84½″ background rectangle to the top of the quilt back.

5. Join the 35½″ × 84½″ background rectangle to the bottom of the quilt back.

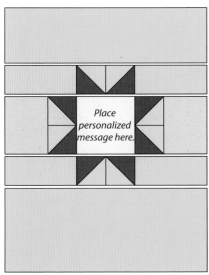

Place personalized message here.

Quilt back assembly

Finishing

Refer to Finishing Basics (page 108) for more detailed instructions.

1. Layer the backing, batting, and quilt top. Quilt as desired.

2. Join the 2¼″ × WOF binding strips into 1 continuous piece for binding. Press, folding the strip in half lengthwise. Sew the binding to the quilt using your preferred method.

Change It Up

Like *Celtic Knot* (page 34), this eight-sided-star quilt is very versatile. It would be perfect for any milestone birthday. It works for many other milestones as well. Maybe someone you love is celebrating an anniversary at work, becoming debt free, starring in a play, or even celebrating years of sobriety. You'd be surprised at the many milestones your loved ones celebrate. Let them know how proud you are!

I Do!

Combine solids and prints in the bride's and groom's favorite colors to commemorate their special day.

QUILT TOP MATERIALS

- Large heart appliqués and Border 3 cornerstone fabric: 1 yard

- Appliqué and block fabrics: ¾ yard each of 9 prints

- Appliqué background fabric: 1¼ yards

- Border 1 fabric: ¼ yard

- Border 2 fabric: ¼ yard

- Border 4 fabric: 1½ yards

- Border 5 and binding fabric: 1⅛ yards

- Appliqué thread, 28 weight: in coordinating colors

- Paper-backed fusible web: 2 yards 18″ wide

- Tear-away stabilizer: 4 sheets* 15″ × 24″

- Batting: 80″ × 80″

If you don't have larger sheets of stabilizer on hand, you can use smaller sheets and overlap them a bit so that they back the entire appliqué area. If you prefer not to use stabilizer, you can heavily starch the background fabric.

Appliqué Shapes

1. Trace the "I Do!" appliqué shapes (pullout page P2) onto the smooth side of paper-backed fusible web. Note: This is a symmetrical design, so follow the notes on the patterns regarding placement and number of copies. Window the fusible (page 105), if desired.

2. Fuse the rough side of the 2 large heart shapes onto the wrong side of the cornerstone fabric. Cut out the shapes on the traced lines.

3. Fuse the rough side of the rest of the shapes onto the wrong side of your choice of appliqué fabrics. Cut out the shapes on the traced lines.

Hint

Cut your appliqué pieces first to ensure that you have enough uncut yardage to accommodate the appliqué shapes *before* cutting the rest of the materials.

FINISHED QUILT: 69½″ × 69½″

Fabrics shown are from the Rosecliff Manor collection by Emily Taylor Design for Riley Blake Designs and Riley Blake solids.

Pieced and quilted by Amanda Murphy

QUILT TOP CUTTING INSTRUCTIONS

From the remainder of the cornerstone fabric:

- Cut 2 strips 6½″ × WOF. Subcut into 8 squares 6½″ × 6½″ for corner-stones. Set aside 4 squares for cornerstones on the quilt back.

From the block fabrics:

- From the remaining fabric, cut a total of 46 squares 7½″ × 7½″, using some of each of the fabrics.

- Cut a total of 36 rectangles 3½″ × 6½″ from the block fabrics.

From the appliqué background fabric:

- Cut 1 strip 39″ × WOF. Subcut into 1 square 39″ × 39″.

From Border 1 fabrics:

- Cut 4 strips 1½″ × WOF. Piece 2 rectangles 1½″ × 38½″ and 2 rectangles 1½″ × 40½″.

From the Border 2 fabric:

- Cut 5 strips 1½″ × WOF. Piece 2 rectangles 1½″ × 40½″ and 2 rectangles 1½″ × 42½″.

From the Border 4 fabric:

- Cut 13 strips 3½″ × WOF. Piece 4 rectangles 3½″ × 54½″. Subcut the remaining strips into 72 squares 3½″ × 3½″.

- Cut 1 strip 7″ × WOF. Subcut into 2 squares 7″ × 7″.

From the Border 5 and binding fabric:

- Cut 8 strips 2″ × WOF. Piece 2 rectangles 2″ × 66½″ and 2 rectangles 2″ × 69½″.

- Cut 8 strips 2¼″ × WOF. Set aside for binding.

WOF = width of fabric

Appliqué Assembly

1. Fold a 39″ × 39″ background square in half in both directions, pressing lightly. Following the quilt top assembly diagram (page 78), arrange the appliqué shapes on the right side of the square. (You can also use the placement diagram on the pullout and a light box or window to align your pieces.) Remove the paper backing and fuse the shapes to secure them.

2. Back the block with tear-away stabilizer and secure the appliqué shapes to the central panel fabric using a blanket stitch. Refer to Appliqué Basics (page 104) as needed.

3. Trim the central block to a square 38½″ × 38½″.

Quarter-Square Triangle Assembly

1. Draw a diagonal line on the wrong side of 23 of the 7½″ × 7½″ squares.

2. Place a marked square on an unmarked square of a different fabric, right sides together, and pin. Sew ¼″ away from both sides of the drawn line. Repeat to sew all the squares together. Set aside 2 sewn units for the Border 4 corner blocks. **Figure 1**

1

3. Cut the remaining units from Step 2 on the drawn line to make 2 half-square triangle units (44 total). Press the seams toward the darker fabric. Keep the cut units together in pairs. **Figure 2**

2

Make 44.

4. Place 2 matching half-square triangle units right sides together, making sure that the seams lock and that the contrasting fabrics are opposite each other. Draw a diagonal line on the wrong side of the top unit in each pair. Sew ¼″ away from both sides of the drawn line. Cut them apart on the drawn line and press the seams open to make a quarter-square triangle unit. Trim to 6½″ × 6½″. Set aside 14 for the quilt back. **Figure 3**

3

Make 42.

5. Join 4 sets of 7 quarter-square triangle units together in rows, pressing the seams open.

Make 4.

6. Join a cornerstone square 6½″ × 6½″ to each side of 2 quarter-square triangle rows, pressing the seams toward the cornerstones.

Make 2.

7. To make the corner blocks, draw a diagonal line across the back of the units set aside in Step 2 (page 76). Lay them on top of the Border 4 background 7″ × 7″ squares, right sides together, and pin. Sew ¼″ away from both sides of the drawn line. Cut the units apart on the drawn line and press the seams open. Trim to 6½″ × 6½″. Set aside these 4 corner blocks. Figure 4

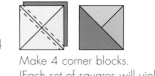

Make 4 corner blocks.
(Each set of squares will yield 2.)

Flying Geese Assembly

1. Draw a diagonal line on the wrong side of each 3½″ × 3½″ Border 4 square.

2. Lay a marked square on the upper right corner of a 3½″ × 6½″ rectangle, right sides together, with the diagonal oriented as shown. Stitch a hairline away from the line, on the side closest to the corner. Trim the seams to ¼″ and press them open. Figure 5

Make 36.

3. Lay a marked square on the upper left corner of the unit from Step 2, right sides together, with the diagonal oriented as shown. Stitch a hairline away from the line, on the side closest to the corner. Trim the seams to ¼″ and press them open. Figure 6

Flying Geese block

4. Repeat Steps 2 and 3 to make a total of 36 Flying Geese blocks.

5. Join the Flying Geese, narrow end to narrow end, to create 4 rows of 9 Flying Geese blocks each. Press the seams open.

6. Join a Border 4 rectangle 3½″ × 54½″ to each Flying Geese strip as shown. Make sure not to cut off the points of the Flying Geese!

7. Join a corner unit from Step 7 (Quarter-Square Triangle Assembly, page 76) to each end of 2 of the 9-block Flying Geese rows as shown. Press the seams toward the center of the corner block.

Quilt Top Assembly

1. Join a 1½″ × 38½″ Border 1 rectangle to both sides of the central block.

2. Join a Border 1 rectangle 1½″ × 40½″ to the top and bottom of the central block.

3. Join a Border 2 rectangle 1½″ × 40½″ to both sides of the central block.

4. Join a Border 2 rectangle 1½″ × 42½″ to the top and bottom of the central block.

5. Join a 7-unit quarter-square triangle row to both sides of the quilt top. Press the seams toward the center of the quilt top.

6. Join a 7-unit quarter-square triangle row with the cornerstone blocks on each end to the top and bottom of the quilt top. Press the seams toward the center of the quilt top.

7. Join a 9-block Flying Geese row to both sides of the quilt top, pressing the seams toward the Flying Geese border.

8. Join a 9-block Flying Geese row with the corner blocks to the top and bottom of the quilt top, pressing the seams toward the Flying Geese border.

9. Join a 2″ × 66½″ Border 5 rectangle to the sides of the quilt top. Press.

10. Join a 2″ × 69½″ Border 5 rectangle to the top and bottom of the quilt top. Press.

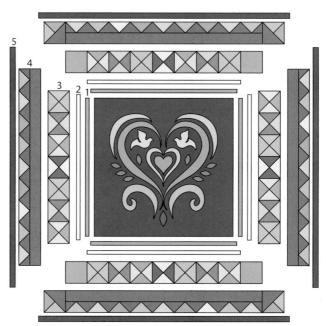

Quilt top assembly

QUILT BACK

79½″ × 84¼″ unfinished
(5″ larger on the sides and
7 ½″ larger on the top and
bottom than the quilt top)

Embroider or print and
transfer the bride's and
groom's names, along
with their wedding date,
on the back of the quilt.

QUILT BACK MATERIALS

- Quarter-square triangles and corner-stones set aside from the quilt top
- Cornerstone fabric: 4 squares 6½″ × 6½″ set aside from the quilt top
- Personalization panel fabric: ½ yard
- Flying Geese "geese" fabric: ½ yard
- Flying Geese "sky" fabric: ½ yard
- Background fabric: 4½ yards
- Tools for personalization (pages 8–10)

QUILT BACK CUTTING INSTRUCTIONS

From the personalization panel fabric:

- Cut 1 rectangle 13½″ × 31½″.

From the Flying Geese "geese" fabric:

- Cut 4 strips 3½″ × WOF. Subcut into 20 rectangles 3½″ × 6½″.

From the Flying Geese "sky" fabric:

- Cut 4 strips 3½″ × WOF. Subcut into 40 squares 3½″ × 3½″.

From the background fabric:

- Cut 2 strips 21½″ × WOF. Subcut into 2 rectangles 21½″ × 37″.

- Cut 1 strip 24½″ × WOF. Subcut into 2 rectangles 24½″ × 19″.

- Cut 2 strips 39½″ × WOF. Subcut into 2 rectangles 39½″ × 37″.

WOF = width of fabric

Personalization

1. Refer to Personalizing Your Quilts (page 7) to add the couple's names and the wedding date, centered on the fabric for the personalization panel, using the method of your choice. *Remember to place text at least ¼″ from all outer edges so it will not be lost in the seam allowances.* For this quilt I used machine embroidery.

2. Trim the panel to a rectangle 12½″ × 30½″.

Center Block Assembly

1. Join 2 sets of 5 quarter-square triangle blocks together into rows, pressing the seams open. Join a 6½″ × 6½″ cornerstone square onto each end of the row, pressing the seams toward the cornerstone squares.

2. Join 2 sets of 2 quarter-square triangle blocks together into rows, pressing the seams open.

3. Join the 2-block quarter-square triangle rows to the sides of the personalized panel, pressing the seams toward the personalized panel.

4. Join the 5-block quarter-square triangle rows to the top and bottom of the personalized panel, pressing the seams toward the personalized panel.

Flying Geese Assembly

1. Referring to the quilt top Flying Geese Assembly instructions (page 77), use the geese rectangles and sky squares to make 20 Flying Geese.

2. Join 7 Flying Geese together, wide end to wide end, to make a 7-unit Flying Geese strip. Press the seams open.

3. Join 13 Flying Geese together, wide end to wide end, to make a 13-unit Flying Geese strip. Press the seams open.

Quilt Back Assembly

1. Join a 19½″ × 24½″ background rectangle to the sides of the personalized panel.

2. Join a 21½″ × 37″ background rectangle to both sides of the 7-unit Flying Geese strip.

3. Join a 37″ × 39½″ background rectangle to both sides of the 13-unit Flying Geese strip.

4. Join the rows.

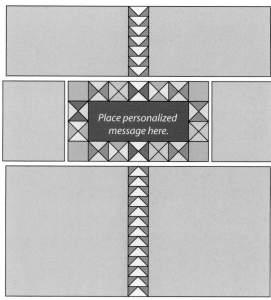

Quilt back assembly

Finishing

Refer to Finishing Basics (page 108) for more detailed instructions.

1. Layer the backing, batting, and quilt top. Quilt as desired.

2. Join the 2¼″ × WOF binding strips into 1 continuous piece for binding. Press, folding the strip in half lengthwise. Sew the binding to the quilt using your preferred method.

Change It Up

If your quilt isn't finished in time to be a wedding gift, this design works beautifully as an anniversary quilt!

A Life Together

Celebrate your years together in style with this modern wallhanging!

QUILT TOP MATERIALS

- Tree branches fabric: ½ yard
- Bird fabrics: 1 fat eighth each of 2 fabrics
- Leaves fabric: 1 fat eighth
- Numbers fabric: 1 fat eighth
- Appliqué background fabric: 1½ yards
- Appliqué border fabric: ⅛ yard
- Wonky Log Cabin block fabrics: 1 fat quarter each of 14–18 fabrics
- Binding fabric: ⅜ yard
- Appliqué thread, 28 weight: in a variety of coordinating colors
- Paper-backed fusible web: 2¼ yards 18″ wide
- Tear-away stabilizer: 2¼ yards 18″ wide, or 3 sheets* 15″ × 24″

If you don't have larger sheets of stabilizer on hand, you can use smaller sheets and overlap them a bit so that they back the entire appliqué area. If you prefer not to use stabilizer, you can heavily starch the background fabric.

QUILT TOP CUTTING INSTRUCTIONS

From the appliqué background fabric:

- Cut 2 strips 11″ × WOF. Subcut into 3 rectangles 11″ × 16″. Set these aside for the back of the quilt top.
- Cut 1 strip 25½″ × WOF. Subcut into 1 rectangle 25½″ × 33″.

From the appliqué border fabric:

- Cut 1 strip 1½″ × WOF. Subcut into 1 rectangle 1½″ × 32½″.
- Cut 1 strip 2″ × WOF. Subcut into 1 rectangle 2″ × 32½″.

From *each* wonky Log Cabin block fabric:

- Cut 1 strip 3″ × 20″. Subcut a *total* of 16 squares 3″ × 3″ and 16 rectangles 3″ × 4½″ from these strips for the block centers.

Cutting wonky strips

- Cut 1 strip 8″ × 20″. Subcut a *total* of 128 slightly wonky strips from these strips for the logs. They should be anywhere from 1¼″ to 2½″ wide × 8″ long.
- Set aside the remaining fabric to use as borders for the appliqué blocks on the back of the quilt.

From the binding fabric:

- Cut 5 strips 2¼″ × WOF.

WOF = width of fabric

FINISHED QUILT: 32½″ × 47½″

Fabrics shown are from the Basics collection by Riley Blake Designs, the Modern Lace collection by Amanda Murphy for Blend Fabrics, and Kona cotton by Robert Kaufman Fabrics.

Pieced and quilted by Amanda Murphy

Appliqué Panel

1. Trace the *A Life Together* branch appliqué shape (pullout page P1) and the leaf and bird appliqué shapes (pages 92 and 93) onto the smooth side of the paper-backed fusible web. (You might have to use masking tape to join a few separate pieces of fusible in order to trace the branch.) Window the fusible (page 105) on the birds, if desired.

2. Trace the appropriate numbers (pullout page P1) onto the smooth side of the paper-backed fusible web.

3. Fuse the rough side of fusible web shapes onto the wrong side of the appropriate fabrics. Cut out the shapes on the traced lines.

4. Following the finished quilt photo (previous page), arrange the branch, bird, and leaf appliqué shapes on the background rectangle. Remove the paper and fuse to secure.

5. Back the fabric with the tear-away stabilizer. Secure the appliqué shapes to the central panel using a blanket stitch, as shown in Appliqué Basics (page 104).

6. Trim the central block to a 25″ × 32½″ rectangle.

7. Join a 1½″ × 32½″ border rectangle to the top of the appliqué block.

8. Join a 2″ × 32½″ border rectangle to the bottom of the appliqué block.

9. Following the quilt top assembly diagram (page 87), arrange the numbers on the appliqué panel. Remove the paper and fuse to secure.

10. Back the panel with the tear-away stabilizer behind the numbers. Secure the numbers to the central panel using a blanket stitch.

Wonky Log Cabin Assembly

1. Trim the top and *right* sides of 16 center squares 3″ × 3″ and 8 center rectangles 3″ × 4½″ at a slight angle so that those edges are a little wonky. **Figure 1**

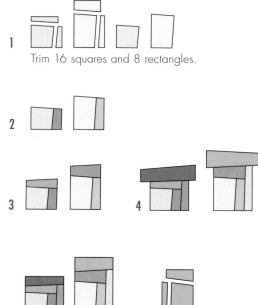

1 Trim 16 squares and 8 rectangles.

2. Join a wonky log strip to the right side of the wonky center squares and rectangles. Press the seams open and trim flush with the block. **Figure 2**

3. Join a wonky log strip to the top of each unit. Press the seams open and trim flush with the center piece. **Figure 3**

4. Repeat Steps 2 and 3 to add 1 more round of wonky log strips to the right side and top of each unit. **Figure 4**

5. Trim the 16 square Log Cabin units to 4½″ × 4½″ and the 8 rectangle Log Cabin units to 4½″ × 6½″. **Figure 5**

6. Trim the top and *left* sides of 8 Log Cabin rectangles 3″ × 4½″ at a slight angle so that those edges are a little wonky. **Figure 6**

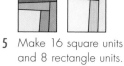

5 Make 16 square units and 8 rectangle units.

6 Trim 8 rectangles.

7. Repeat Steps 2–5, this time adding strips to the top and *left* side of each wonky center rectangle, to make 8 mirror-image rectangle Log Cabin units 4½″ × 6½″. **Figure 7**

8. Join 2 square wonky Log Cabin units as shown, pressing the seams toward the right. Repeat this step to make a total of 8 half-blocks. **Figure 8**

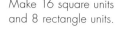

7 Make 8 mirror-image units.

8 Make 8.

9 Make 4 wonky Log Cabin blocks.

9. Join 2 half-blocks together as shown to make a wonky Log Cabin block. Repeat this step to make a total of 4 blocks. **Figure 9**

10. Join the 4 blocks together to form an 8½″-high wonky Log Cabin row. **Figure 10**

10

11. Join 1 rectangle wonky Log Cabin unit and 1 mirror-image rectangle wonky Log Cabin unit, pressing the seams toward the right. Repeat this step to make a total of 8 half-blocks. **Figure 11**

12. Join 2 half-blocks together as shown to make a wonky Log Cabin block. Repeat this step to make a total of 4 blocks. **Figure 12**

13. Join the 4 blocks together to form a 12½″-high wonky Log Cabin row. **Figure 13**

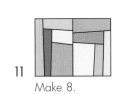

11   Make 8.

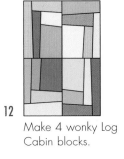

12   Make 4 wonky Log Cabin blocks.

13

Quilt Top Assembly

1. Join the 8½″-high wonky Log Cabin row to the top of the appliqué block.

2. Join the 12½″-high wonky Log Cabin row to the bottom of the appliqué block.

Quilt top assembly

QUILT BACK

42½″ × 57½″ unfinished
(5″ larger on all sides than quilt top)

Embroider or print and transfer the husband's and wife's names, along with their wedding date, on the back of the quilt.

QUILT BACK MATERIALS

- Appliqué and wonky block fabrics set aside from the quilt top

- Background fabric: 1¾ yards

- Accent strip fabric: ⅓ yard (or ⅞ yard if using a directional print running the length of the fabric)

- Appliqué thread, 28 weight: in a variety of coordinating colors

- Paper-backed fusible web: ¾ yard 18″ wide

- Tear-away stabilizer: 1 yard 18″ wide, or 3 sheets* 15″ × 24″

- Tools for personalization (pages 8–10)

If you don't have larger sheets of stabilizer on hand, you can use smaller sheets and overlap them a bit so that they back the entire appliqué area. If you prefer not to use stabilizer, you can heavily starch the background fabric.

QUILT BACK CUTTING INSTRUCTIONS

From the remaining wonky Log Cabin block fabrics:

- Choose the prints you would like to use for the appliqué block borders. Cut a total of 12 strips 3″ × 20″ from these prints.

From the accent strip fabric:

> ### Note
> If you are using a directional print, you may want to cut the following pieces lengthwise and piece them.

- Cut 2 strips 5¼″ × WOF. From the strips, piece 1 rectangle 5¼″ × 57½″.

From the background fabric:

- Cut 1 strip 2½″ × WOF. Subcut into 2 rectangles 2½″ × 17″.

- Cut 1 strip 9¾″ × WOF. Subcut into 2 rectangles 9¾″ × 17″.

> ### Note
> If you are using a directional print, you may want to cut the following pieces lengthwise and piece them:

- Cut 2 strips 4¼″ × WOF. Piece into a rectangle 4¼″ × 57½″.

- Cut 2 strips 8¾″ × WOF. Piece into a rectangle 8¾″ × 57½″.

- Cut 2 strips 9¼″ × WOF. Piece into a rectangle 9¼″ × 57½″.

WOF = width of fabric

Appliqué Panels and Personalization

1. Trace the portions of the branch shape (pullout page P1) and some leaves and the two birds (pages 92 and 93) from the *A Life Together* patterns onto the smooth side of the fusible web. Window the fusible (page 105) on the birds, if desired.

2. Fuse the rough side of the shapes onto the wrong side of the appropriate fabrics. Cut out the shapes on the traced lines.

3. Following the quilt back assembly, arrange the appliqué shapes on the 3 appliqué background rectangles 11″ × 16″.

4. Refer to Personalizing Your Quilts (page 7) to add your unique message on one of the appliqué panels, using the method of your choice. For this quilt I used machine embroidery to note the names and wedding date of the couple. *Remember to place text at least ¼″ from all outer edges so it will not be lost in the seam allowances.*

5. Refer to Tips and Techniques (page 104) to back the appliqué panels with tear-away stabilizer. Secure the appliqué shapes to the central panel using a blanket stitch.

6. Trim the panels to 10″ × 15″.

7. Trim a little bit more off of each edge to make the panels wonky. Don't overdo it here—less is more!

8. Join a 3″ × 20″ appliqué border strip to each side of the appliqué panels, trimming off the excess each time.

9. Trim the blocks to 12″ × 17″ rectangles.

Quilt Back Assembly

1. Join the 3 appliqué blocks with 2 background rectangles 2½″ × 17″ to form the quilt back center.

2. Join a 9¾″ × 17″ background rectangle to the top and bottom of the quilt back center.

3. Join a 4¼″ × 57½″ background rectangle to the left side of the quilt back center.

4. Join a 9¼″ × 57½″ background rectangle to the right side of the quilt back center.

5. Join the 5¼″ × 57½″ vertical stripe rectangle to the left side of the quilt back center.

6. Join the 8¾″ × 57½″ background rectangle to the left side of the quilt back center.

Finishing

Refer to Finishing Basics (page 108) for more detailed instructions.

1. Layer the backing, batting, and quilt top. Quilt as desired.

2. Join the 2¼″ × WOF binding strips into 1 continuous piece for binding. Press, folding the strip in half length-wise. Sew the binding to the quilt using your preferred method.

3. If desired, make a narrow hanging sleeve from remaining fabric and hand stitch the sleeve to the back of the wallhanging.

Quilt back assembly

A Life Together
Bird 1

Trace 1 for the front and 1 for the back.

Change It Up

Remove the number and add a reduced-size bird between the pair on this quilt, and what a darling baby quilt you'd have, particularly nice for an adoption! Or instead of the numbers, place a bird in the lower left corner and the idea that these birds are saying goodbye is not far-fetched, making it a great going-away quilt. These appliqué shapes would be at home in any quilt—maybe a bird on a branch would be just right for your *Welcome to the World!* quilt. Let your imagination soar.

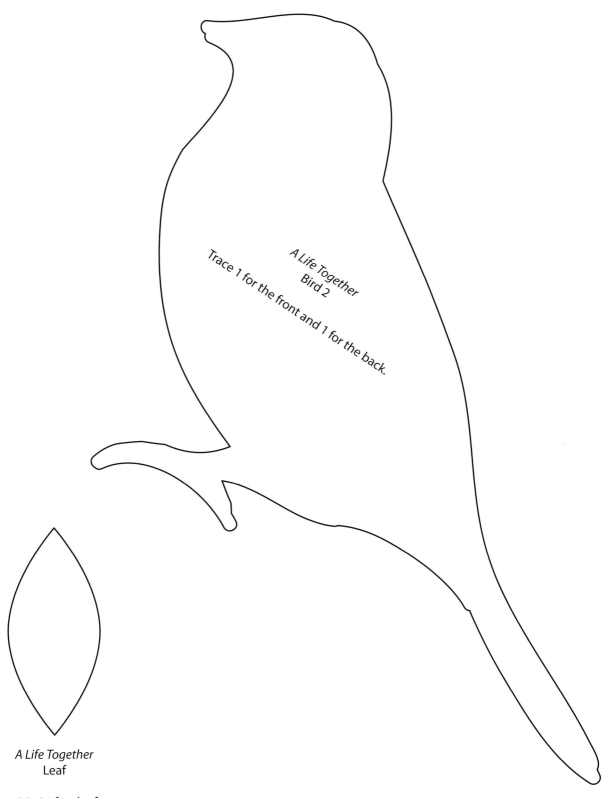

A Life Together
Bird 2
Trace 1 for the front and 1 for the back.

A Life Together
Leaf

Trace 20–24 for the front.
Trace 20–24 for the back.

We Remember...

As long as people live in our memories, they are not forgotten. This quilt is inspired by a vast landscape, and it also symbolizes the spiritual journey throughout our lives.

QUILT TOP MATERIALS

- Earth fabrics: 1 yard each of 4 different brown prints
- Air fabrics: ¾ yard each of 4 different cream prints
- Cloud fabrics: ¾ yard each of 4 different salmon prints
- Sky fabrics: 1 yard each of 4 different aqua prints
- Arrowhead fabric: 1 yard white solid
- Binding fabric: ⅝ yard
- Batting: 75″ × 102″

QUILT TOP CUTTING INSTRUCTIONS

From *each* of the earth and sky fabrics:

- Cut 2 strips 4½″ × WOF. Set these aside for the back of the quilt. (One will be extra.)
- Cut 4 strips 4½″ × WOF. Subcut into 4 rectangles 4½″ × 28½″.

Note

If any of your fabrics are directional and the design runs parallel to the selvage, you might want to cut the strips lengthwise.

- From *each* of the sky fabrics (but not the earth fabrics), cut 12 squares 2½″ × 2½″. Of these, set 4 squares of *each* fabric aside for the back of the quilt.

WOF = width of fabric

Cutting continues (page 97)

FINISHED QUILT: 64½″ × 91½″

Fabrics shown are from the Winged collection by Bonnie Christine for Art Gallery Fabrics and Kona cotton by Robert Kaufman Fabrics

Pieced and quilted by Amanda Murphy

CUTTING INSTRUCTIONS CONTINUED

From *each* of the air and cloud fabrics:

- Cut 4 strips 4½" × WOF. Subcut each strip into 1 rectangle 4½" × 28½".

Note

If any of your fabrics are directional and the design runs parallel to the selvage, you might want to cut the strips lengthwise and piece them to achieve the desired length

- From the remaining fabrics, cut 2 squares 2½" × 2½" from each print (8 total).

From the arrowhead fabric:

- Cut 6 strips 2½" × WOF and 3 strips 4½" × WOF. Subcut the 2½" × WOF strips into 96 squares 2½" × 2½" and the 4½" × WOF strips into 48 rectangles 2½" × 4½".

From the binding fabric:

- Cut 9 strips 2¼" × WOF.

Flying Geese Strips

1. Draw a diagonal line on the wrong side of all the 2½″ × 2½″ arrowhead and earth, air, cloud, and sky squares. (For any directional prints, make sure the diagonal line is oriented one way on half of the squares and the other way on the other half. Set them aside in matching pairs.)

Note: All the earth, air, cloud, and sky strips and Flying Geese units will be oriented vertically in the quilt top and horizontally in the quilt back. Both are constructed in the same way.

2. Lay a 2½″ × 2½″ arrowhead square on the right top corner of each of the 4½″-wide cloud, air, and earth strips, orienting the diagonal line as shown. Sew right on the diagonal line. Trim the seams to ¼″ and press open. **Figure 1**

3. Lay a 2½″ × 2½″ arrowhead square on the left top corner of each of the 4½″-wide cloud, air, and earth strips, orienting the diagonal line as shown. Sew right on the diagonal line. Trim the seams to ¼″ and press open. **Figure 2**

4. Lay a square from each pair of 2½″ × 2½″ sky, cloud, or air squares on the top right corner of each of the 4½″ × 2½″ arrowhead rectangles, orienting the diagonal line as shown. Be careful that any directional prints are oriented correctly! Sew right on the diagonal line. Trim the seams to ¼″ and press open. **Figure 3**

5. Lay the matching square from each pair of 2½″ × 2½″ sky, cloud, or air squares on the top left corner of each of their respective arrowhead units, orienting the diagonal line as shown. Be careful that any directional prints are oriented correctly! Sew right on the diagonal line. Trim the seams to ¼″ and press open to make a total of 48 Flying Geese units. **Figure 4**

6. Join the long strip you completed in Steps 3 and 4 to a matching Flying Geese unit from Step 5. **Figure 5**

1

2

3

4

5

Quilt Top Assembly

1. Join an earth, air, cloud, and sky unit into a long column. Repeat to form 16 columns.

2. Stagger the columns until you are pleased with their appearance. While you want to stagger them, a general trend upward looks nice. Trim the columns from each end as shown so each is 91½″ long. **Figure 6**

3. Join the columns.

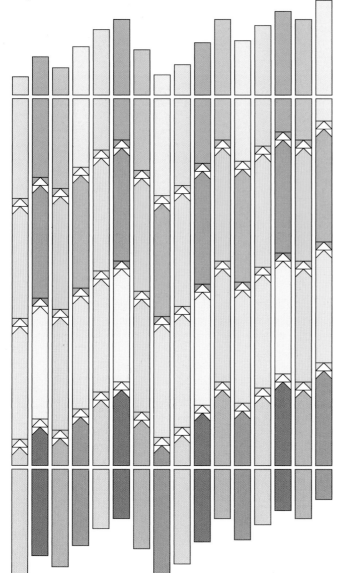

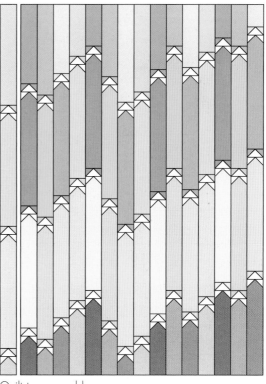

Quilt top assembly

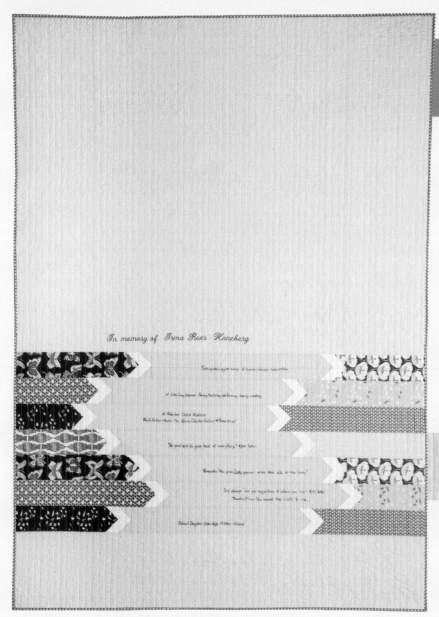

QUILT BACK

74½″ × 101½″ unfinished
(5″ larger on all sides than
quilt top)

Mail strips of fabric to your
loved ones so that they can
record their favorite memories
for posterity. The following
directions are for incorporating
7 strips of memories, but
you can add more, as desired.

QUILT BACK MATERIALS

- Remainder of the 4½″ × WOF sky and earth strips set aside when cutting the quilt top
- Sky squares 2½″ × 2½″ set aside when cutting the quilt top
- Background fabric: 4¼ yards
- Memory strip fabric: 1¼ yards light solid
- Arrowhead fabric: ½ yard
- Fabric-marking pens (I like Fabrico pens.)
- Tools for personalization (pages 8–10)

QUILT BACK CUTTING INSTRUCTIONS

From *each* of the earth and sky strips:

- Trim off the selvages to yield a rectangle 4½″ × approximately 40″.

From the memory fabric:

- Cut 1 strip 2½″ × WOF. Subcut into 14 squares 2½″ × 2½″.

- Cut 7 (or more) strips 5″ × WOF. Subcut each into a 5″ × 32″ rectangle.

From the arrowhead fabric:

- Cut 1 strip 2½″ × WOF. Subcut into 28 squares 2½″ × 2½″.

- Cut 2 strips 4½″ × WOF. Subcut into 14 rectangles 4½″ × 2½″.

From the background fabric:

- Cut 2 strips 17½″ × WOF. Subcut into 1 rectangle 17½″ × 40″ and 2 rectangles 17½″ × 17¾″.

- Cut 2 strips 56½″ × WOF. Subcut into 1 rectangle 56½″ × 40″ and 2 rectangles 56½″ × 17¾″.

Personalization

1. Send the 5″ × 32″ memory strips to friends and family, along with fabric-marking pens and a copy of Handwriting (page 9) so they can record their favorite memories of your loved one and send them back to you. Make sure they know not to write within ½″ of the top and bottom and to start writing at least 3″ from the left edge of the strip!

2. Trim each strip to 4½″ × 28½″.

3. Refer to Personalizing Your Quilts (page 7) to create your unique message, such as "In memory of _____," using the method of your choice in a coordinating dark color that reads well against the background fabric. Depending on where you choose to place the message, it can be applied now or after the background fabric has been pieced. I used Lesley Riley's TAP Transfer Artist Paper (from C&T Publishing) and inkjet printer. *Remember to place text at least ¼″ from all outer edges so it will not be lost in the seam allowances.*

Flying Geese Strips

1. Draw a diagonal line on the wrong side of all the 2½″ × 2½″ arrowhead memory, earth, and sky squares. (For any directional prints, make sure the diagonal line is oriented one way on half of the squares and the other way on the other half. Set them aside in matching pairs.)

2. Trim the memory strips to 4½″ × approximately 28½″–40″. (Make sure the writing starts at least 2½″ from the left raw edge and doesn't come within ¼″ of the top and bottom edges.)

3. Refer to the quilt top instructions for Steps 2 and 3 of Flying Geese Strips (page 98) to sew 2 arrowhead squares to the right-hand end of 7 memory and 7 earth strips as shown. The completed strips will be oriented horizontally in the quilt back but are constructed the same as in the quilt top. **Figure 6**

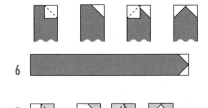

4. Refer to the quilt top instructions for Steps 4 and 5 of Flying Geese Strips (page 98) to sew a pair of 2½″ × 2½″ sky squares to each of 7 arrowhead rectangles 4½″ × 2½″. **Figure 7**

5. Join a Flying Geese unit from the previous step to the left-hand ends of the matching sky and memory strips. **Figures 8 and 9**

Place sentiments of affection here.

Quilt Back Assembly

1. Join an earth unit, a memory unit, and a sky unit into a long row. Repeat to form 7 rows.

2. Stagger the personalized rows until you are pleased with their appearance. Trim each row to 74½″ wide. Join the rows.

3. Join a 17½″ × 17¾″ background rectangle to each side of the 17½″ × 40″ background rectangle.

4. Join a 56½″ × 17¾″ background rectangle to each side of the 56½″ × 40″ background rectangle.

5. Join the top and bottom background sections with the personalized rows to form the quilt back.

6. Refer to the quilt assembly diagram to place and transfer any personalization text onto the quilt back. Make sure that the text starts at least 10″ from the raw edge of the quilt back.

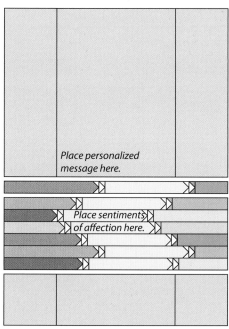

Quilt back assembly

Finishing

Refer to Finishing Basics (page 108) for more detailed instructions.

1. Layer the backing, batting, and quilt top. Quilt as desired.

2. Join the 2¼″ × WOF binding strips into 1 continuous piece for binding. Press, folding the strip in half lengthwise. Sew the binding to the quilt using your preferred method.

Change It Up

This is the perfect memory quilt to personalize. It can easily be a graduation quilt with strips signed by friends and family. Or how about a retirement quilt with all the retiree's colleagues writing a comment or two?

Tips and Techniques

Experiment with different types of fusible web to find what works best for your project.

APPLIQUÉ BASICS

1. Trace the desired shapes onto the smooth side of paper-backed fusible web. If you are tracing a large shape, you can trace smaller shapes inside it to cut down on waste.

2. Cut shapes apart roughly.

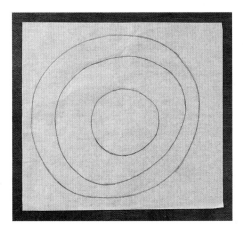

Windowing

If you would like to reduce the stiffness of your finished appliquéd piece, consider windowing. *Windowing* is cutting away any excess fusible from within your appliqué shape, leaving at least ¼″ of fusible around the inside edge of the shape. It is essential if are working with a heavier-weight fusible but optional if you are using a very lightweight fusible. It is also helpful to eliminate the bulk in projects that feature several appliqués layered on top of each other, as you are able to easily cut away the background layers of shapes that have been secured using this windowing technique.

3. Fuse the shapes to the wrong side of the fabrics and cut out the shapes on the traced lines.

4. Remove the paper and arrange the shapes as desired on the background fabric. Fuse them to secure.

5. Cut a piece of tear-away stabilizer that is at least 1″ bigger than the appliqué area on all sides. Back the block with tear-away stabilizer. If using fusible stabilizer, follow the manufacturer's instructions to fuse it to the wrong side of the block. If using regular tear-away, use a light coating of spray adhesive to

attach it—too much leaves a residue. I like OESD Tear Away Stabilizer, which comes in a variety of widths and weights. You can also heavily starch the background fabric if you prefer not to use stabilizer.

6. Use a blanket stitch in 28-weight thread to secure the outermost appliqué, making sure to decrease your thread tension so that the bobbin thread doesn't pop up to the top. (You can also use 50-weight thread, but I like the ridge that a slightly thicker thread produces.) Bring the threads to the back and knot them. Clip the threads, leaving ¼″–½″ tails.

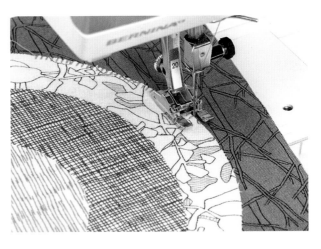

7. Remove the stabilizer, trying to keep the circle intact. (You can score the edge of the stabilizer right along the stitch-ing line with a pin or chenille needle to make this easier.) Cut out the background fabric from behind the largest circle to prevent fabric buildup.

8. Back the piece with the circle of stabilizer you just removed.

9. Repeat Steps 6–8 to attach the medium and small circles.

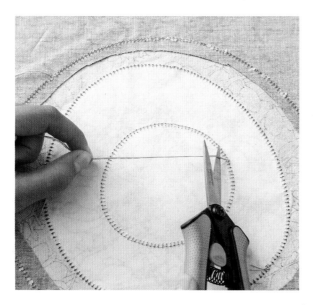

Appliqué Stitches

The two appliqué stitches I tend to use most frequently are the blanket stitch and the invisible hem stitch.

For most raw-edge appliqué I like to use the blanket stitch in 28-weight Aurifil thread. This stitch is number 1329 on my BERNINA 780, with a stitch width of 2.1 and a stitch length of 2.4. I use 50-weight in the bobbin and lower my thread tension so that my bobbin thread does not pop up to the top of the quilt top.

For machine appliqué that has a folded edge, like a bias strip, I like to use the subtle invisible hem stitch in the top and bottom, with standard machine settings.

Finally, for really small-raw edge appliqué pieces, like for circles under ¾″ in diameter, I usually opt to use a narrow zigzag stitch in 50-weight thread.

For more appliqué tips, look for my Craftsy (craftsy.com) appliqué class on Craftsy (see Resources, page 110).

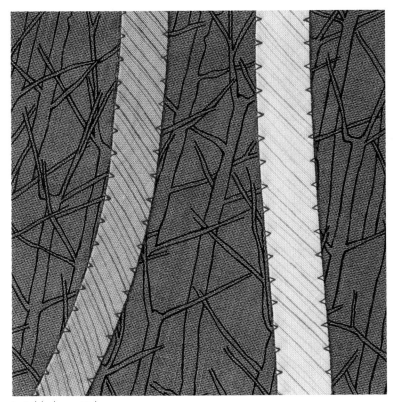

Invisible hem stitch

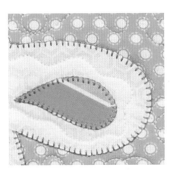

Blanket stitch

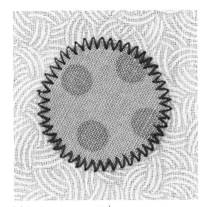

Narrow zigzag stitch

FINISHING BASICS

Borders

When you have finished the quilt top center, measure it through the middle vertically. This will be the length to cut the side borders. Piece the strips together to achieve the needed lengths. Cut the longest pieces needed first; then use remaining strips for shorter borders. Place pins at the centers of all four sides of the quilt top, as well as in the center of each side border strip. Pin the side borders to the quilt top first, matching the center pins. Sew the borders to the quilt top and press the seams toward the border.

Measure horizontally across the center of the quilt top, including the side borders. This will be the length to cut the top and bottom borders. Repeat the process of pinning, sewing, and pressing.

Backing

Plan on making the backing a minimum of 8″ longer and wider than the quilt top. Piece your backing fabric if necessary. I include instructions for pieced backs at least 10″ larger than the top for all the quilts in this book.

Batting

These quilts feature Warm & Natural or Warm & White cotton batting. Cut the batting approximately 8″ longer and wider than your quilt top.

Layering

Spread the backing wrong side up and tape the edges down with masking tape. (If you are working on carpet you can use T-pins to secure the backing to the carpet.) Center the batting on top, smoothing out any folds. Place the quilt top right side up on top of the batting and backing, making sure it is centered.

Basting

Basting keeps the quilt "sandwich" layers from shifting while you are quilting.

If you plan to quilt with a domestic sewing machine, pin baste the quilt layers together with safety pins placed about 3″–4″ apart.

Quilting

Quilting, whether by hand or machine, enhances the pieced or appliquéd design of the quilt. You may choose to quilt in-the-ditch, echo the pieced or appliqué motifs, use patterns from quilting design books and stencils, or do your own free-motion quilting. Remember to check your batting manufacturer's recommendations for how close the quilting lines must be.

Binding

Trim the excess batting and backing from the quilt even with the edges of the quilt top.

If you want a ¼″ finished binding, cut the binding strips 2¼″ wide and piece them together with diagonal seams to make a continuous binding strip. Trim the seam allowance to ¼″. Press the seams open.

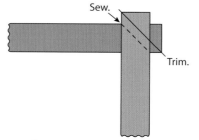

Sew from corner to corner.

Completed diagonal seam

Press the entire strip in half lengthwise with wrong sides together. With raw edges even, pin the binding to the front edge of the quilt a few inches away from a corner, and leave the first few inches of the binding unattached. Start sewing, using a ¼″ seam allowance.

Stop ¼″ away from the first corner (see Step 1), and backstitch one stitch. Lift the presser foot and needle. Rotate the quilt one-quarter turn. Fold the binding at a right angle so it extends straight above the quilt and the fold forms a 45° angle in the corner (see Step 2). Then bring the binding strip down even with the edge of the quilt (see Step 3). Begin sewing at the folded edge. Repeat in the same manner at all corners.

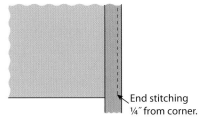

Step 1. Stitch to ¼″ from corner.

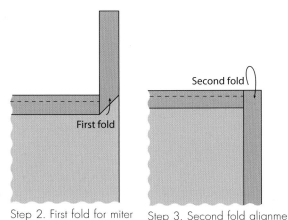

Step 2. First fold for miter   Step 3. Second fold alignment

Continue stitching until you are back near the beginning of the binding strip. Cut both ends of the binding so that they overlap a scant 2¼″.

Open both tails. Place one tail on top of the other tail at right angles, right sides together. Mark a diagonal line from corner to corner and stitch on the line. Check that you've done it correctly and that the binding fits the quilt; then trim the seam allowance to ¼″. Press open.

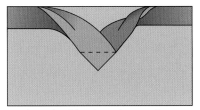

Stitch ends of binding diagonally.

Refold the binding and stitch this binding section in place on the quilt. Fold the binding over the raw edges to the quilt back and hand stitch.

For instructions on making continuous bias binding, please consult my blog at blog.amandamurphydesign.com or C&T Publishing's website at ctpub.com > search "continuous bias binding."

Resources

FABRIC DESIGNERS

Bonnie Christine
goinghometoroost.com

Carolyn Friedlander
carolynfriedlander.com

Carina Gardner
carinagardner.com

Amanda Murphy
amandamurphydesign.com

Emily Taylor Design
emilytaylordesign.com

Lila Tueller
lilatuellerdesigns.blogspot.com

Angela Walters
quiltingismytherapy.com

SUPPLIERS

Art Gallery Fabrics
artgalleryfabrics.com
artgalleryfabrics.typepad.com/weblog

Aurifil USA
aurifil.com
auribuzz.wordpress.com

BERNINA of America, Inc.
berninausa.com
weallsew.com

Blend Fabrics
blendfabrics.com

Craftsy
(20 Fresh Appliqué Techniques, Amanda's online appliqué class)
craftsy.com/instructors/
amanda-murphy

C&T Publishing
(Lesley Riley's TAP Transfer Artist Paper; Create with Transfer Artist Paper, *by Lesley Riley; Essential Sandboard from Piece O' Cake Designs)*
ctpub.com
ctpub.com/blog

OESD / Oklahoma Embroidery Supply & Design
(Tear-away stabilizers)
embroideryonline.com
blog.embroideryonline.com

Riley Blake Designs
rileyblakedesigns.com
rileyblakedesigns.com/blog

Robert Kaufman Fabrics
robertkaufman.com
swatchandstitch.com

The Warm Company
(Warm & White and Warm & Natural batting)
warmcompany.com

About the Author

Always attracted to color, texture, and pattern, Amanda Murphy has been designing, drawing, and sewing since she was a child. After graduating with a bachelor of fine arts degree in design from Carnegie Mellon University, she worked as a graphic designer and art director in Alexandria, Virginia, and in New York City. After moving to North Carolina with her family, Amanda discovered quilting, an art that marries her passion for design with her enthusiasm for handwork. As she gradually expanded her knowledge of quilting techniques and combined them with the ideas she had been sketching over the years, Amanda Murphy Design was born.

Amanda markets her own pattern line under the Amanda Murphy Design label and has designed several fabric collections, most recently for Benartex. This is her fourth book for C&T Publishing, following *Modern Holiday*, *Color Essentials*, and *Free-Motion Quilting Idea Book*. Amanda is also a BERNINA quilting and longarm spokesperson and teaches quilting classes on Craftsy (craftsy.com).

Amanda hopes her books, fabrics, and quilt designs will inspire others to create their own works of art. Visit her websites and share designs you make from this book.

Post pictures of your *Quilted Celebrations* projects using the hashtag #quiltedcelebrations

Photo courtesy of BERNINA of America Inc.

Website: amandamurphydesign.com

Blog: blog.amandamurphydesign.com

Facebook: amandamurphyfabrics

Instagram: amandamurphydesign

Pinterest: pinterest.com/amdfabrics

Flickr group: flickr.com/groups/amandamurphy_sewing_patterns

Craftsy profile: Amanda Murphy

OTHER BOOKS BY AMANDA MURPHY:

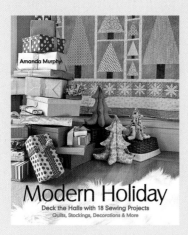

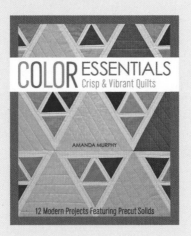

Visit us at **ctpub.com** and receive a special offer

For inspiring content that keeps you smiling and sewing

Find out what's new at C&T PUBLISHING

FREE Projects ▪ FREE How-to Videos

Blog ▪ Books ▪ Patterns ▪ Tools ▪ Rulers

Templates ▪ TAP Transfer Artist Paper

kraft•tex™ ▪ & more

Go to ctpub.com/offer

Sign up and receive your special offer